ROAD
OF AGES

ROBERT NATHAN

ROAD
OF AGES

❊

ALFRED · A · KNOPF
NEW YORK
1935

Therefore fear thou not, O my servant Jacob, saith the Lord; neither be dismayed, O Israel: for lo, I will save thee from afar, and thy seed from the land of their captivity; and Jacob shall return, and shall be in rest, and be quiet, and none shall make him afraid.

For I am with thee, saith the Lord, to save thee: though I make a full end of all nations whither I have scattered thee, yet will I not make a full end of thee: but I will correct thee in measure, and will not leave thee altogether unpunished.

Behold, I will bring them from the north country, and gather them from the coasts of the earth, and with them the blind and the lame, the woman with child and her that travaileth together; a great company shall return there. They shall come with weeping, and with supplications will I lead them; I will cause them to walk by the rivers of waters in a straight way, wherein they shall not stumble.

JEREMIAH.

ROAD
OF AGES

THE JEWS WERE GOING into exile. Eastward across
Europe the great columns moved slowly and with
difficulty toward the deserts of Asia, where these unhappy people, driven from all the countries of the
world, and for the last time in retreat, had been offered a haven by the Mongols. At night their fires
burned along the Danube, or lighted the dark Bakony
forests; while the wooded reaches of the Tisza echoed
with the tramp of feet, the creak of carts, the purring
of motors, and conversation in all the languages of
the world.

Their columns spread across the desolate Hungarian plains, and crossed the frontiers of Czecho-
Slovakia. Whole villages marched together, led by
their rabbis; and with them rode or walked the rem-

—3—

nant of the race, men and women who had once been
citizens of all the nations of earth. They went slowly,
for many of them were on foot, and almost all of
them had lost their possessions. They carried with
them a few sheep, a few goats, the treasures of the
synagogues, and a little household furniture.

It was a strange looking army which toiled eastward toward the mountain passes. The new world
and the old met and embraced with caution in the
shadow of exile. Pushcarts piled high with bedding,
covered wains, ox-carts, and motorcycles crowded
each other along the roads on which an entire people
moved, drawn from the four quarters of the globe.

As they advanced they were joined by refugees
from Roumania, Hungary, and Jugoslavia. New
voices, harsh with excitement and fatigue, mingled
with the voices of the west, of France, of Germany,
and of England. They were given food; they took
their places in the line, and faced the unknown which
awaited them.

They had many enemies; and few if any friends.
In order to defend themselves, they had organized

a battalion of soldiers under the command of an English general of brigade. Equipped with pistols, old carbines, deer guns, and fowling pieces, veterans of the wars and young men out of college patrolled the line of march, and fought off robbers, and bands of students from the universities.

Already, since they had started, some had been killed, and others wounded. But they were used to suffering, and they were not afraid to die. Anxious, alert, hungry, and weary, they followed their leader, the aged Nieman, who rode in the van, or returned thoughtfully along the line of march, a journey of more than fifty miles.

As he passed, accompanied by the general, Lord Steyne, or by Dr. Hart, the rabbi, there arose from every side cries of enthusiasm or of protest. For the Jews had not been made over by their misfortunes; it was impossible for them, even at this time, to agree with one another. Beaten by students, robbed by the peasants, and assaulted by the police of every country, they nevertheless, in the midst of their distress, kept alive their differences of opinion.

They were dissatisfied because they were being led to Asia, and not to Palestine. They would have liked to return to Zion, to live a life of glory again. But Jerusalem also had been taken away from them; they had not been able to retain that tiny strip of seacoast, so vital to the world's great empires. Those dry hills, those not-too-fertile valleys, the tombs of Saul and David, belonged to England. In the whole world there was no land poor enough for the Jews. Only the Gobi was offered them; and so to the Gobi they went. But not without many arguments and discussions.

As the army rested for the night in the warm and silent plains, or in the windy passes of the hills, these discussions continued around the camp-fires, where the high sweet songs of the girls mingled with the sound of dances, the one-step and the czardas, violins and accordions, tangos from Cuba, and waltzes from Berlin.

While their elders argued, the young people danced. They were ardent and unhappy; the mystery of life, the danger of death, touched and dismayed them. The distant barking of dogs, the sweet night smells, the dark and secret land beyond their wagons, filled their hearts with longing, and with a never-ending excitement. Already there were disputes about the new state which was to arise in the east; and men could be seen shaking their fists at each other over the question of profits and public owner-ship. But for the most part, the young people danced in the firelight.

In the daytime the children played along the road, gathering the flowers of the region to make chaplets for their hair. They alone were without care or anxiety; and they fought over again in miniature the battles of their elders. The little girls in rompers or cotton dresses pretended to be nurses, and consoled with bandages of moss and pills made of acorns their wounded brothers and cousins. Only, at night before they fell asleep, they sometimes played at house, remembering drowsily the homes in which they had lived, warm and secure, and surrounded by their treasures.

And when, as sometimes happened, little Germans whose parents had been beaten to death, cried out with terror in their sleep, French hands patted the pillow, American voices hushed them, Polish lullabies comforted their dreams.

In the morning they had forgotten their grief, and smiled happily over their breakfast, which often consisted of nothing but water.

For supplies were meager, and it was difficult to procure food along the way. Those who had money bought what they could, and gave each day a small share to those who had nothing. Some who owned a pistol or a shotgun, went hunting for rabbits, or birds; while the poor begged, or even stole, despite the orders of their leaders, who did not wish to offend the peasants. This order aroused a great deal of discussion.

"Are we to go hungry?" asked the wife of the Kovnitz Rabbi, gazing anxiously at her empty kettle. For the rabbi had left to his wife the problem of feeding his family, and also his followers, who tramped in the dust behind the rabbinic carriage.

The women were the quartermasters of this army.

They saw to it that the small supply of milk was portioned out to the children; they kept the stew-pots filled with whatever was to be had; and gave to everyone what was due him, either for his wealth, or for his effort; or out of the sympathy of their natures.

Smiling, unable to understand the words they addressed to one another, the women of England and Jugoslavia spoke together in the language of soups, stews, and cold boiled leeks and vegetables.

On Friday evening the Tabernacles were set up in the fields, or beneath the trees, where those who wished to worship sat or knelt on the grass, and in the misty evening air, under the fading sky, intoned their immemorial prayers, and wept for the dead. Night, darkening in the east, found them still praying in the dew, the smoke of their fires ascending like a sacrifice toward heaven.

At the same time others who did not wish to pray, engaged in games of chance, in pinochle and whist, and in concerts on the violin. A thousand activities occupied the Jews on the march. Even the needle trades were busy, for many garments had to be altered for travelling. There was work for everyone, although there was not very much money with which to pay for it. As the army neared the frontiers, bankers made change from one currency to another; doctors and surgeons attended to the public health; and in the fields there were songs and speeches, and classes in Hebrew and political economy.

There also the doctors of philosophy from Oxford and Heidelberg disputed with their friends from Padua, Yale, Grenoble, and Beirut. While the army toiled eastward in the midst of danger, in the parching sun, and through torrential rains, they debated with energy the polarity of the cell, the meaning of history, and the value of metaphysics. But they had no laboratories; and the scorpions with which the biologist Eischenheim had hoped to establish the dimorphism of the egg, perished in the forests of Czecho-Slovakia.

It was autumn, the time of the Jewish holidays; and the trees were already beginning to die. At night the air was cold; and mists rose from the meadows, and from the ponds in which frogs kept up a melancholy croaking. The shofar, the great ram's horn, blown by the Chief Rabbi of Galicia, had sounded the new year; and from the ovens came fragrant cakes, and apples dipped in honey. The white mantles for the scrolls of the Law were drawn out and aired, to be ready for Yom Kippur; and the children dressed in silk, or in calico, wished their parents a happy new year, and made their own shy wishes on the moon, or on the first faint stars, silver and doubtful in the sky.

The army lay in the village of Jasina, and on the roads and fields to the west, in the direction of the Hungarian border. There the Jews rested for the holidays; and also to enable the sick and the wounded to catch up with them. Dr. Wasserman's hospital was at Beregsasy; he was obliged to move slowly with his patients, many of whom were suffering from ulcers of the stomach, brought about by the uncertain conditions of the march. He had with him, as assistant, Dr. Paul Kohn, and the latter's Christian wife, Amanda Nichols. She shared her husband's exile; and hid as well as she could the dismay she felt among so many strangers.

During holy week, Lord Steyne and his soldiers patrolled the roads about Jasina. With him went the liberal rabbi, Dr. Hart, to minister to the soldiers. Orthodox Jews drew aside their praying shawls as he passed, erect and clean-shaven, among them. He did not mind; in his melodious and at the same time powerful voice, he recited from the Psalms, and blessed the people. Nevertheless as he stood with his head thrown back, and his hands upraised, he was aware of the fact that the English industrialist, Mr. Solomon, was not paying any attention to him.

The sun shone down, the yellow autumn light lay like a benediction on the Jews, busy about their wagons, or slumbering in their tents. The light, high voices of children, like the piping of swallows, rose from among the leaves fallen on the grass; the sound of chanting, and the clink of an anvil, mingled together in the daytime air. Little by little the sun sank westward in the sky; the shadows lengthened in the fields, the blue light of day faded from the

air; and in the clear green heavens, shining like a
lamp, the young curved moon, the moon of the new
year gazed down on Israel.

2

FRANCES NINIAN, in her seventy-third year, climbed slowly down from the cart in which she had been taking a mid-day nap, into the dry fields of Czecho-Slovakia. Her silver hair was crowned with a small bonnet of straw, decorated with ribands; and her sweet face, lined and wrinkled with age, expressed energy and joy, due to a healthy body and a friendly disposition. There was time before evening prayers for a game of cards, or for a walk with her friend Mrs. Blumenthal; and she felt the need of amusement of this kind.

Since the army was no longer moving, she found herself growing a little fretful. Mrs. Blumenthal, who had just passed her eightieth birthday, also preferred to be on the march. They wished to live long enough to see the new land, and to experience fresh sensations; they wanted to feel, once again, their roots, the roots of their families, taking hold in the soil. To camp, without conveniences, in the fields of middle Europe, did not seem to them a very exciting thing to do; although at the same time they were glad to rest for a little while.

As they walked slowly together through the motors and wagons, the tethered oxen, the sheep and the donkeys, they exchanged greetings with the wife of the Kovnitz Rabbi, and bowed politely to the French banker, M. Paul Perez, and his family. They would have liked to talk to Mrs. Liebkowitz, the rabbi's wife; but they knew no Yiddish, and she spoke no English. And Mme. Perez, seated in the rear of her limousine, spoke only French. She respected the elderly ladies from America; but they did not interest her.

She was reading, for the third time, M. Théophile Gautier's *La Chaine d'Or;* and capturing for herself, again, though more and more faintly, the odor of Paris in the fall, dead leaves and motors along the

Avenue des Champs Élysées, the faint, sour smell of wine from the cafés, the scent of perfumes from the shops in the Faubourg St. Honoré. Surrounded by the aromas of camp, the smell of fires and dung, of soap and cooked food, she remembered with all her might the fragrance of her boudoir on the Avenue Friedland; and how, in the evening, the lamps were lighted, and the curtains drawn, and all the world shut out, except that little part of it—that part of Paris—which she loved.

Now, among strangers, in the midst of fields ripe for the harvest, she kept what elegance she could; and still surprised at what had happened to her, remained polite, and remote from those around her. She had no lover; the Member of the Chamber of Deputies with whom, for many years, she had enjoyed a discreet and comfortable intimacy, had stayed at home where he belonged, among his vineyards in the Touraine. She often wondered, gazing about her with bright, birdlike glances, what woman, as yet unknown, would initiate her son Raoul into the fulness of life, supposing always that it were not too late to initiate him at all . . . or at least console him on the march, and direct his ambitions.

If she thought at all about the strange land to which she and her family were moving among so many others, it was to envisage a city in which, at evening, lamps were lighted, and curtains drawn; and where, upon a couch before the fire, men and women exchanged confidences of a tender, or a political nature.

But with Mrs. Ninian, and Mrs. Blumenthal, she did not desire to exchange anything at all, beyond the respect due to their years; for she felt no greater curiosity about America than she did about the Gobi Desert.

And as they passed, she returned to her book, to M. Théophile Gautier, who spoke the language of her heart, clear, formal, and indulgent, like Paris, like that city which she loved.

The two old ladies went by among the goats and the wagons, past Polish mothers in their shawls, and Latvian men with beards. As they walked slowly through the dusty grass, breathing the mild air in which there was already a hint of cold, they exchanged wordless smiles of greeting with their fellow travellers. But their thoughts were with Mme. Perez, remote and elegant in her motor car. "I feel so sorry for her, Mary," said Mrs. Ninian, closing her eyes to rest them from the sun. "She must feel so alone among us."

Mrs. Blumenthal had been alone too, in her life. "I was never very happy in Paris," she remarked. "I was always glad when it was time to get on the boat, to come home."

And she was silent, remembering that she had no home to return to any more.

"Don't let's walk too far, Frank," she said at length. "I'm not as young as I was."

"Nonsense," replied Mrs. Ninian briskly. "You mustn't think such things." Nevertheless, she looked anxiously, and sidewise at her friend; and after a moment added:

"Let us sit here and rest for a while."

They settled themselves on a mound of grass at the edge of the road. Around them stretched the wide and yellow fields; while far off in the east, blue against the sky, the rude hills still to be crossed gazed down upon them. Along the road, as far as they could see, the Jews had pitched their camps, eastward toward Jasina, and westward toward Hungary. Smoke rose in the air; and the wandering clouds of autumn trailed their shadows over the mountains, and across the fields.

"It's peaceful here," said Mrs. Blumenthal, looking around her.

She sat, her brown old fingers holding her friend's hand, her cloudy eyes fixed on the distant mountains toward which she was being led, those mountains which were some day to rise again behind her, to shut her off forever from the world in which she had been born.

"I wonder will we live to cross those mountains, Frank," she said.

"We'd better," answered Mrs. Ninian firmly; "that's all I've got to say."

"Nobody wants to more than I," said Mrs. Blumenthal. She was afraid of dying, of being left

— 19 —

behind, buried in a strange field, among alien people—lost in grass over which no children would ever play the games she knew, or lovers talk together in a language she could understand.

Mrs. Ninian, on the other hand, had no fear at all. For one thing, she was too busy; for she had not only herself to look after, but also her grandson, the poet, David Weiss. She was not too old to do her own cooking; and what with the joys and troubles of the march, the new sights to be seen each day, the work to be done, if not for herself, then for others—to say nothing of her game of cards in the evening—life was too full and active to let her think very much about death. Only, sometimes, in the rain, or if she awoke at night, her heart beat a little with fear . . . she was, after all, near the end of her days, and there was still a long way to go across the earth.

"We'll be in Russia before Christmas," she told her friend. "And then we won't have so much fighting."

"There'll be snow in Russia," said Mrs. Blumenthal. Mrs. Ninian agreed that it would be cold.

"Though we'll be in the south," she added doubt-fully.

Mrs. Blumenthal looked to the east, to the hills; but her old eyes saw only a distant blur of blue. "I never thought," she said, "that my husband and I wouldn't be buried together."

Her own daughter had died long ago, at home. And in the riots she had lost others of her family. But there were still a few left—enough perhaps, to keep a grave green and tended. . . .

"What a rest we'll have when we get there, Frank," she said.

"Not a bit of it," said Mrs. Ninian briskly. "There'll be more to do than ever. And I'm glad of it.

"For you know, my dear," she added, leaning over to pat her friend's hand, "our generation was never taught to do nothing.

"That was left for those who came after us."

She liked women to be busy, to be happy, and not to have too good a time in the world. Her principles were those of her mother before her: to tend the sick, feed the poor, and keep a tidy house. Toward men, and toward God, she maintained a respectful attitude, lightened by the belief that in a crisis she could deal adequately with either of them.

"Yes," she said again, "there'll be lots to do." And she thought of charities to be organized, of sewing to be done, of recipes for cooking to be exchanged. "I wonder if we shall have a city to live in," she said, "and what it will look like."

"China, perhaps," replied Mrs. Blumenthal, since they expected to be near Mongolia.

That made it seem so far away. Their hearts sank; and they sat for a moment without speaking. "Well," said Mrs. Ninian at last, "it's time we were getting back."

They rose, with an effort, and started back through the lines to their own wagons. The afternoon sun was falling steeply in the sky; the shadows in the yellow, dusty grass were long and slanting. Far off in the east the hills took on a deeper tone, as the sky behind them deepened also. The evening cooking had begun; the sound of women over their stoves flowed like a tide around the wagons, pierced by an occasional cry, the laughter of children, and the lowing of cattle. And under it, closer yet to earth, the voices of cricket and cicada kept up their troubling song.

Mrs. Ninian had supper to get for herself and her grandson. Not that there was much to do . . . there was a little stew left from the day before, and she had bought some milk from a farmer a few miles back. David had gone to buy a lettuce, if possible; and to ask for a little oil from Mr. Solomon, the merchant, who was in charge of supplies.

He was returning now, with the oil and the lettuce. And his thoughts, as he walked along, spread themselves dreamily around the slender figure and golden hair of Betty Solomon, the merchant's daughter. She had a little gramophone, on which she played over and over again the dance records of the winter before, her first year as a debutante in society. David would have liked to talk to her, he had even made up in his mind the things he would have liked to say. And he imagined how she would answer, in a sweet and friendly manner. But actually, her answers were vague, or angry; and made him feel awkward. She was not very friendly; he did not know what she wanted.

Still, there wasn't any doubt about it, she was pretty to look at—like an English girl to whom nothing ever happened.

That was what was wonderful, he thought: to live in a world in which nothing ever happened.

Presently he forgot her again, watching the deepening shadows on the hills; and his thoughts faced the future with courage and joy. The past was behind him; he need never go back to it. Ahead of him was the fresh new day, in which everything was possible—even peace, even wisdom. Let the Jews carry the light from the old world, dark with hate, sick with torment, into the new . . . the light of peace, of love, of kindness, along with the Ark, their silver ornaments, and their household bedding. The night, deepening beyond the hills, spread itself like a fog in the sky; but already, beyond the night, eastward, beyond the darkness, the sun was making ready to rise again; already, on the other side of the earth, its golden light touched the blue waters of the Pacific.

Lost in dreams of glory and of peace, he stopped to speak to his friend Raoul Perez, whom he observed seated on a wagon-tongue at the edge of the camp. The banker's son was staring moodily before him, a look of bewilderment upon his face, which ordinarily expressed only doubt, sensibility, and disdain. At sight of the poet, holding his lettuce, and a little oil in a bottle, his expression grew brighter; and he exclaimed with energy; "Where have you been?"

David let himself down onto the wagon-tongue, stretching out his legs for balance in the grass. "Well," he said comfortably, "the Holidays are nearly over; we'll soon be on the march again. Will you be glad, do you think? And your parents? I shall be, for one."

The young Frenchman shrugged his shoulders. "My mother does not care where we go," he said, "and my father is busy, I do not see him. As for me, yes, I would like to get to the end of this march; but I am happy here."

And he gazed with a sigh in the direction of the Kovnitz wagons.

David smiled; for he knew that his friend was thinking of Leah Liebkowitz, the daughter of the Kovnitz Rabbi, with whom he was in love. He had lost his heart to her in the great plains of Hungary, as she walked beside her parents, a shawl over her hair. That was a month ago; and he had not yet spoken to her. Yet he knew that she had seen him; and he believed that her heart also trembled and rejoiced.

"It is fate," he explained to David. "Although," he added, "I do not think my parents will give their consent.

"Nevertheless," he concluded mournfully, "I am very happy."

And he was silent, staring at the darkening hills, where night gathered.

"My friend," he said at last, "where are we going? To what land, where we shall be able to live as our spirits tell us? Already I see, in imagination, my home in the Gobi Desert. It is like the apartment of a friend of mine in the Rue du Boissy. The question is, will Leah feel at ease in such surroundings? At all events, we will bring up our children to speak French."

"Where we are going," said David dreamily; "if one only knew . . . But there are many endings to this journey, Raoul. One road leads to the synagogue, another leads to a bank. We are like the twelve tribes, all enemies together. Some think of wealth, others of society; some wish to fight, and others to run away. I myself do not know what I want, because I am not a practical economist."

"You are a communist," said Raoul; "or, at least a socialist."

And standing up, he yawned, and stretched his arms above his head. "For me," he explained, "I am a royalist.

"Vive le roi."

The two friends returned through the camp, through the blue dusk of evening, Raoul in the best of spirits, David with his lettuce and his little bottle of oil. When he arrived at the fire over which his grandmother had hung her pot of stew, he said to her,

"I have brought Raoul Perez home to supper with us."

"He's welcome to what we have," said Mrs. Ninian.

MR. AND MRS. HYMAN COHEN had owned a little delicatessen store on Columbus Avenue in New York City. Now they had their belongings on a pushcart; and Mrs. Cohen was expecting a baby. Not for a long time yet, not until April; but she was already a little frightened. It seemed to her that the warm Hungarian plains, the moonlit nights, the singing, and the sense of danger everywhere, had served to betray her. She wished that she had a few women friends to talk to; they were mostly foreigners in her part of the line, she didn't know anybody, except to smile at, or to say a few words to around the fire of an evening.

Hyman wasn't much help to her either, in that way. Thin, small, with watery blue eyes, he pushed his barrow along the road all day, and at night he was too tired to go any further. But he saw everything for the best, he believed that everything would turn out all right. And he assured Madelon that in the new state they would have a big circle of acquaintances. "You will see," he said; "everybody will be friends there with everybody else. Even the rich will give up some of their wealth, because they will be obliged to, by the government."

But he only hoped, after all; and Madelon wanted more than hope, she wanted comfort.

"How can I live?" she cried. "I would like to lie down and die right now, only then what would happen to me?"

"Don't even say such a thing," said Mr. Cohen; "just when we're getting along so well. . . ."

"So well?" replied Madelon. "Without a place to sleep? Without clothes for my back? Without even friends?"

Mr. Cohen sighed. He, too, was lonely; in his younger years, before he was married, he had been a socialist. Then he had had friends—lots of them;

they argued and talked together until late into the night. And there were parades, and meetings. And then, later, when he owned a delicatessen, people would come in for a bottle of beer, or a pickle, and stay on to discuss things—the state of the country, people's health, anything at all—what a joy it was to talk, to be friendly with everybody. Democrats— even Republicans—there was always something to say.

"Eh?" he asked, for he realized that Madelon had been talking to him.

"I said I am hungry," said Mrs. Cohen. "You should look somewhere for supper, Hyman. What I also said was, will there be milk in the new land? A desert; does that sound like milk?"

"Milk?" he cried heartily; "why of course. Everywhere in the world are cows. You will see; in April it is spring, and everywhere is milk."

And with an awkward pat on her shoulder, he turned away to see what he could find for supper in the pots and kettles of more fortunate neighbors.

He filled the bottom of his bowl with soup from

the big kettle of Baron Wertheim of Vienna. The rule of the march was charity; the leaders of the divisions were expected to see that no one actually starved. Mr. Cohen would have liked to hang his own pot over a fire, but at the moment he had nothing to put in it.

The same was true of many others. Back toward the town of Huste, Oscar Alberg, once a leader of the Amalgamated Clothing Workers of the World, wandered among the fires of his division, from which ascended smoke, sparks, and savory odors. He was looking for someone with whom to share his evening meal; toward which he was ready to donate a small lettuce, given him by Mr. Solomon. A company of fugitives had just come in from the north; weeping and arguing, they were being settled for the night among the already crowded carts and wagons. Mr. Alberg made his way around them until he reached the Kovnitz fires; then, hurrying forward, he said to Mrs. Liebkowitz, the rabbi's wife,

"We are in luck; somebody gave me this fine lettuce."

So saying, he held out the little bunch of green to the rabbi's wife, who felt that she could not accept it without asking him to sit down with them at supper.

A moment later, to his satisfaction, Mr. Alberg found himself at table with Leah, the brown-haired daughter of the Kovnitzer. She sat in the firelight, silent and dreamy, her eyes fixed not so much upon the fire, or the gloom beyond, as on some slight and inner flame. She was young; yet she had lived through history. She had seen men die; she had wept with women in their despair. In the darkness of her day, the little lamp of love gave out a gentle light, beyond which she did not wish to look. She thought of Raoul, with whom she had not yet exchanged a word; she thought of marriage, and of a home with her parents, like the home they had left in Kovnitz. There she would forget, as her ancestors had forgotten, the dreadful experiences of life; and learn, as they had learned, to make gingerbread, and almond cakes.

And in imagination, shyly, and with modesty,

she saw herself lighting the candles in her own home on the sabbath eve, while her husband prepared himself to recite, in her honor, the thirty-first chapter of Proverbs.

That the husband of whom she dreamed had never in his life recited so much as the benediction before the sabbath meal, did not even cross her mind.

Her silence was not a matter of concern to her parents, who would have been surprised and displeased if she had been more lively. A silent and loving woman, the rabbi often said, quoting Ben Sira, is a gift from the Lord. But Mr. Alberg found her presence no less disturbing for being so modest. The privacy of her thoughts, the secrecy of her body, intruded themselves upon his world—that world in which nothing was either secret or private. And confused and unhappy, he struggled to keep from desiring, for himself alone, that warm and appetising property; and tried to keep his mind upon the larger issues which were of an economic and ethical nature.

"What," he exclaimed, "when we arrive in China, are the bankers to own everything again, as they did before? I tell you, it is out of the question. Who is our leader? A capitalist; and the director of a bank. Not any more, of course; but he was."

"We are not yet anywhere near China," replied the rabbi mildly; "so do not let us worry about the bankers. As for our leader—if you mean Mr. Nieman—that is a term which does not signify anything. God, Blessed be He, is our leader; as well as the Chief Rabbis of England, Poland, Austria, and Lithuania."

When Mr. Alberg was alone, he did not hesitate to snap his fingers at God. But he did not wish to vex the rabbi, whose daughter sat beside him in the firelight.

"Well," he said finally, "of course—God— hmm . . ."

And with a deep sigh, he filled his mouth with lettuce.

"What do you think, Miss Leah?" he asked her shyly.

But Leah remained silent; she did not seem to hear him. And he continued with energy;

"We will build a new world, in which the poor people and the workers will own everything, and where everybody will have an entire room to live in."

The rabbi gazed at his wife; he remembered the wide and rambling house at Kovnitz, the rabbinic court with its many rooms; and he heard what Mr. Alberg was saying. With a strong shudder, he replied:

"Do not think of such a thing."

"It is already a fact," replied Mr. Alberg.

At this Leah, clasping her hands softly together, suddenly exclaimed: "It will be lovely."

For at the thought of living all her life in a single room with Raoul, her heart was filled with excitement and happiness.

"Yes, yes," cried Mr. Alberg gratefully, "it is the young people who will make the new world possible. They alone do not ask for anything for themselves."

And with burning cheeks, he lifted his eyes from the girl's young knees, outlined beneath her skirt.

"Why do we give away our money," he asked hoarsely, "to a few old men who do not do any work? Shall I tell you what they do with it? They send it to other countries; and when we want it back again, it is gone. So then we can go to war for it, if we like. To make this war, we must pay a great deal. Afterwards comes more money, for relief. However, by that time we are already corpses."

"Just the same," said Mrs. Liebkowitz, who so far had said nothing, "it is the bankers who make the money; and for that reason we cannot get along without them."

The rabbi shrugged his shoulders. "Since when," he asked, "do women argue at the supper table as though they were men?"

"Excuse me," said Mrs. Liebkowitz, and relapsed into silence; but not before she had added under her breath,

"Without money what can you do?"

The rabbi then replied to Mr. Alberg:

"When David went forth against the Philistines, he took from them sheep and kine, gold and silver, and he remarked, 'these are my spoils.' With the same treasure, Solomon later built the Temple at Jerusalem. It is said, 'Man will hereafter be called to account for depriving himself of the good things which the world lawfully offers.' It is clear to me that wealth is blessed by the Lord, and that God does not wish everybody to live in one room."

Mr. Alberg was ready to reply to this speech, which caused him to tremble with indignation. But at that moment, suddenly in the darkness, at one corner of the camp, there was heard a cry of terror. It was a sound which froze into ice the blood in people's veins; they turned pale, and rose uncertainly to their feet. Then, in the breathless silence which followed, while they strained to listen, hearing loudest of all the beating of their own hearts, shouts arose, cries for help in Yiddish and German, mingled with Slavic oaths and exclamations in the border languages. In the firelight a few resolute figures could be seen running in the direction of the disturbance; while others seemed to shrink back, to huddle together in the shadows. The Rabbi of Kovnitz gazed helplessly and with terror at his family; he put out his arms as though to gather them to his bosom. But the young communist, Oscar Alberg, seizing a knife from the table, jumped to his feet and hurried in the direction of the disturbance. He was almost happy not to have to talk any more, but to be running as hard as he could to do something.

Far down the road, toward Jasina, a detachment of Lord Steyne's troops started back in a motor car, its siren wailing. This eerie sound, the rush of the motor through the wind and the dark, aroused everyone's fear; and all along the line of march, men stood before their fires, peering anxiously into the darkness, and exchanging low-voiced questions. What had happened? Was it a student raid? Was it an attack by soldiers? Were they all to be killed? Stand firm, Jews with trembling hearts . . .

Mrs. Ninian was already unwrapping gauze to be made into bandages. Her hands shook, but her eyes were bright and sparkling. She was only afraid that she might not be useful enough. Mme. Perez, on the other hand, lay huddled on the plush cushions of her limousine, weeping with loneliness and horror. Where was her little boudoir on the Avenue Friedland, the warm and cosy light, the drawn curtains? Where was her husband? Where was Raoul?

Raoul was safe; he was seated under a tree, wiping the blood from a cut on his cheek, and sniffling with rage. The enemy, some ruffians of the region, were retreating across the fields, with an occasional shot, or a flung stone, to remember them by. They carried their booty with them, a few copper pots, some furs, and a little silver; and left behind them half a dozen Jews with wounds of one sort or another. Among them was Oscar Alberg; he lay on his side, with blood trickling from his mouth. "I'm all right," he said weakly. "Just get me back to the doctors at Beregsasy. It hurts inside.

"I'm used to it," he added grimly, thinking of the riots at home.

And he clenched his hands, to keep from crying out.

Raoul drove him to Beregsasy in his mother's car. There he left him with Doctor Kohn, and returned to his own camp, in which the excitement was slowly dying down. He found his mother sitting pale and composed upon a camp-chair, in the company of a family from Bordeaux, with whom she had not yet exchanged any conversation. After he had led her back to the car, and made her comfortable for the night, he said to her,

"I shall make a little promenade of duty about the camp, to see that all is well."

A single tear upon his mother's cheek was her only answer.

Nevertheless, arming himself with a wagon-spoke, he went off in the darkness, in the direction of the Kovnitz wagons. Mme. Perez ceased to shudder, and prepared herself for sleep. She wished that her husband would come; but she did not expect him. She was relieved to know that he had not been in the fighting; and imagined that he was probably with his friend, Mr. Solomon, or with Mr. Nieman, far ahead.

As a matter of fact, M. Perez was not aware of what had happened. He had gone earlier in the evening to talk over a matter of importance with Baron Wertheim of Vienna; and now, seated in an ox-cart a mile away, he was discussing with his friends a scheme to bring capital into the new land. He saw it as the land of promise; and he wished to make sure that when the time came, the Jews would be in a position to profit by their opportunities.

His spirit was anxious, but his mind was alert; and he expected the firm of Perez to do as well as it could for itself.

"Gentlemen," he said, "I am to tell you that the French bankers are ready to help us. I have lately received letters from Paris to this effect. They are willing to sell, in the Bourse, the shares of such utilities, mining companies, and railroads as we are able to provide them. They ask one thing, in addition to their fee, which is large; that we name our companies, insofar as possible, by titles sympathetic to the French public. I give you as an example, the Franco-Mongolian Compagnie D'Electricité et Distribution, Societé Anonyme."

"Hear, hear," said Mr. Solomon. "Though I

rather fancy," he added, "something like the Mid-
lands Electric, Ltd., myself. That would fetch them
in the City."

"The French bankers," continued M. Perez
quietly, "are ready to guard their interests. Would
the English, in the event that we found ourselves in
difficulties with our neighbors, fight upon the side
of their investments?"

"Well," said Mr. Solomon doubtfully, "they
might, you know."

"Or the Austrians?" asked M. Perez, turning to
Baron Wertheim.

The Baron shrugged his shoulders. "Do not talk
nonsense, my friend," he said. "Those days are long
ago over."

"Then," said M. Perez, "let us count upon Paris."

And with the yellow beams of a lantern lighting
their intent and serious faces, they put their heads
together over decimals and percents.

A mile away in the darkness, Raoul Perez, his
wagon-spoke across his knees, sat on guard before
the Kovnitz wagons. The fires were dying out; in

their fading glow, he could distinguish the black
bulk of the cart in which his Leah slept, with her
mother and her father. Around him the crickets sang
with little voices; an ox moved restlessly against its
halter, a voice spoke faintly in the distance, and was
still again. The odors of the night crept around him,
sweetened by the smoke of fires; and the dark night
wind moved with its cold in the branches above him,
under the sky whose stars bent down upon the silent
wagons and the dreaming youth their shy and shining glance.

He thought of his home, of his sunny childhood
in the Touraine; of Paris, in the rain, in the dusk.
Why had he been driven from France, which he
adored? And Leah—so young, so tender. . . .
What had they done to deserve such a fate? His
eyes filled with tears; and he gripped his wagon-
spoke more tightly.

To be sure, there was tomorrow, and the new
land . . . what was it David always said? The sun
is already up, in the east. Well let it shine there for
a while. Tonight his heart had business in the past,

at home, in France, among the roses. One by one he counted over the treasures of his childhood—the clover meadow in which he had so often played, his dog, his little pony, the house in which he had lived, the winding river, small and mysterious; counted them over in silent anguish, held them out to the brown-haired love in the darkness—offering to the ghost of the child in Kovnitz the long-dead joys of the child in France.

Tomorrow—tomorrow he would make his home in the new land. That would be beautiful, too; it would have its own beauty. He would help build a city, like Paris, with wide avenues, and bridges across a river, with cafes, and theaters, and shops.

But that was tomorrow.

And in her wagon, stretched on a blanket between her parents, Leah smiled in her sleep, dreaming not of Kovnitz, of the great house with its kitchens and offices, but of a single room, built like a little bird cage she had once loved, all of bamboo and of gold. In two days it would be Yom Kippur, the Day of Atonement; she would hear the Kol Nidre sung in the fields, and her sins would be forgiven her. She had nothing to fear. Her warm mouth curved in her sleep; she dreamed of joy.

OSCAR ALBERG lay on a wooden cot in a house in Beregsasy, covered by a cotton blanket. Next to him was stretched a kosher butcher from Galicia, who had been badly hurt in the fighting near Buda; and on the other side, a broker from Hamburg, whose leg had been cut off with a scythe at the Austrian border. Like so many of the exiles, they were penniless; and bitter, not so much at the world, as at each other.

"What I say is this," declared the butcher; "when Jews eat pork, they're done for."

He spoke in Yiddish, thereby making himself understood by Mr. Alberg, but not by the German, or Amanda Nichols, who was in charge of the hospital in which her husband, Dr. Kohn, was assistant director.

"What kind of a leader is that," he added, "who does not even follow the laws of diet? He will never get us to where we are going, by eating everything on the way."

Mr. Alberg replied between groans: "There is no place for superstition when it is a question of feeding so many people."

"What," exclaimed the butcher; "do you speak of superstition? So that is how it is. Well, do you think we will get there without God's help? Or is God perhaps a superstition? You are not a Jew; you are a pork eater, who has come along to destroy us. May you rot; and all others like you."

So saying, he turned his back on Mr. Alberg, and gazed gloomily at the wall.

The broker from Hamburg, clearing his throat, addressed Mr. Alberg in German. "He is a swine," he said, pointing to the butcher. "It is all I can do to keep my patience."

"Let murder be done," remarked the Galician in muffled tones from the bed.

"What I would like to know," continued the

broker, "is this: why was it necessary to bring along with us such people as that? They are everywhere to be seen, pushing and shoving their way. . . . This army is nothing but a rabble. It is not to be endured. In addition, they give us a bad name."

"Then you do not believe that we are all brothers here together?" asked Mr. Alberg.

To this the broker simply replied, "With whom am I to live?"

"With your family, perhaps," said Mr. Alberg, drowsily, and wishing to be left alone.

"My family," said the broker, "no longer exists. Wife, mother, father, uncles—they are all gone. Some were shot by the Nazis; others were beaten to death; a few simply disappeared. I am alone."

"Then be glad," said Mr. Alberg, "that you are safe." And feeling his ribs, he uttered a cry of pain.

"I am a German," said the broker simply, "and I leave Germany with regret. It was a system which I loved and admired. Here everything is too lax, too disorderly. It is my hope to return to Germany again, to the Fatherland, where I belong, where everything is strong and orderly."

Amanda did not understand either of her patients. But then, she did not understand any of the Jews—not even Paul, her husband; not entirely, she thought. And she knew him better than anyone else in the world. No, she was not a stranger any more to the Jews; they did not frighten her any longer. It was only that she knew she could never really belong to them. They were so alive; life was so rich in them, so rising, so restless, it blew so hot-and-cold, glowing and paling, never still, never quiet . . . They aroused her, they moved her; but some essence of their spirit forever escaped her. She was like a tree blowing in the wind; after the wind had passed, she would stand in the sun again, alone, as before.

They were the wind, blowing forever over the earth. And in the wind went the seeds which grew, and the waters which nourished; and the dry leaves of despair. The bitter, life-giving wind. . . .

It was raining when David Weiss came to see

Alberg in the hospital. The march had begun again; and Dr. Wasserman had moved his patients on to Huste. There, in the single street of the little town with its church at one end, and the cemetery at the other, among puddles of water, mud, and drenched piles of manure, he had found a deserted market, and had received permission from the *starotsa* to occupy it for the space of three days. "It's not much," he said, looking at the dark and muddy shed, "but we can at least take the chill off the air." He was afraid to let the column get too far ahead of him; he wished he might have stayed at Beregsasy.

Dr. Kohn's brown young face, usually so amiable, was set in sober lines. "It's bad luck," he said; "the rain. That means snow, up in the passes."

"I know," said Dr. Wasserman with a sigh. He was a great surgeon; he had perfected an operation for embolism. It called for infinite delicacy, and incredible speed; he had never expected to find himself in Czecho-Slovakia.

"We'll have to get through before it gets deep," he said. "Perhaps we'd better push on before the three days are up. If those duodenal ulcers can stand it."

"They'll have to," said his assistant.

Dr. Wasserman's was not the only hospital in the army. But the others were further forward, at Jasina, with Lord Steyne and Mr. Nieman. Like the one at Huste, they suffered from a lack of instruments, medicines, and nurses. The doctors did as well as they could; but they could not keep the Jews from dying.

David Weiss had brought to Huste a woolen muffler and a jar of jelly, the gifts of Mrs. Ninian to Mr. Alberg. She did not know him; it was enough for her that he had been hurt in the fighting. The communist received them in silence, and without expressing a gratitude he did not feel. In the midst of attacks of pain, he put the muffler carefully away for future use; and devoured the jelly by himself.

"Ah," said the butcher, gazing at him; "you have rich friends."

Mr. Alberg did not reply, but ate his jelly as rapidly as possible.

David turned away from the bed. He had come to Huste much against his will; it had been a long ride, in the rain; he was tired and wet, and he wanted to get back again. There was his motorcycle outside, borrowed from Nelson, the prize-fighter—Young Kid Nelson, born Benny Abrams. And Raoul was waiting for him . . . and supper. . . .

Still, he felt obliged to say something to Mr. Alberg, who, having finished his meal, had settled back on the pillow again, ready to talk. On the other hand, he did not know how to begin.

So he remarked stiffly,

"You are a brave fellow. My grandmother hopes that you will get well soon."

"It is nothing," said Mr. Alberg. "I will live to wave the red flag over Mongolia."

"I hope not," said David, buttoning up his coat again, before going out into the rain.

"Why not?" asked the communist. "Do you want to see the flag of Germany floating there, instead? Or the Union Jack? Or perhaps the red white and blue of the United States, or of France. If we sell Jerusalem to the bankers, let us at least wave their flags. Is that what you want? Or perhaps you are a socialist; and do not know what you want."

"No," said David; "I am not a socialist, either."

And he added irritably to himself, under his breath;

"How can I tell you what I want?"

"Before that happens," said Mr. Alberg, with quiet satisfaction, "blood will flow."

"I tell you, I am tired of blood," shouted David suddenly, and turned to go.

Dr. Kohn, walking among the beds nearby, heard him and hurried over. "Look here," he said, taking David by the arm, "this won't do."

At the same time, the wounded man from Hamburg raised himself on his elbow, and shook his fist in David's face. "Why do you shout?" he demanded. "You are disturbing me. You are without manners."

"I'm sorry," said David in a low voice. Turning to the doctor, he murmured, "Forgive me, I am a little upset. I'll be going now."

And he started for the door, beyond which the rain was falling steadily.

"Wait a minute," said Dr. Kohn more gently. "Don't be in a hurry. Sit down; and collect yourself. Have you far to go?"

"We're up ahead," replied David. "About twenty miles. But that's all right—I've a motorcycle."

"I suppose you're with Solomon's crowd," said the doctor thoughtfully. "You ought to be getting near the hills. Is there snow there yet?"

And as David still moved uncertainly toward the door, he added, "Look here—you're tired and cold. Stay and have a cup of tea with us, won't you. You can tell me what things are like, ahead."

"The roads are pretty crowded," said David doubtfully.

"All the more reason to warm yourself first," said the doctor. "You can see that."

"Yes," said David. He looked at the other's brown and friendly face. "Well," he admitted, "perhaps you're right. It's very kind of you. I will, then. Thank you."

Wet, muddy, and very much vexed with himself, David followed the doctor down the street to the inn, where Amanda was already awaiting her husband's return from the hospital.

5

THE TILED RUSSIAN STOVE warmed the air of the
room in which Dr. Kohn lodged with his family, and
at the same time boiled the water for tea. There were
cups for the doctor, his wife, and their guest; and one
cup for their young daughter Ann to share with her
little friend, Alex Wolf. Ann and Alex were too
small to be in love, but old enough to be pleased
with each other; and in addition, there were not
many children to play with. Alex's father had been
in the paint business in New York; because no one
had been willing to buy his factory, he had lost
everything. He travelled slowly, with his little family, as near as possible to Dr. Wasserman, whom he
had known at home; and hoped, if he were careful,
to reach the promised land, and to manufacture
paints again.

"There is always something," said Dr. Kohn, "to keep men alive, some drive of will in a worn out body. With the cold weather still ahead of us, one would think that the old and the sick would be afraid to go on. As a matter of fact, very few of them have a chance of surviving the winter."

David thought of his grandmother, and sighed. "They love life, too," he said in a low voice.

Amanda gazed quickly and shyly at this muddy young man, who so far had said very little. He was not as strong, she thought, nor as vigorous, as her husband; yet he spoke of life as though it were something to which the Jews, also, had a right in the world.

Dr. Kohn was explaining that he took, each morning, a cold bath, where it was possible.

"It's the best tonic in the world," he said.

"Well, tell me," he added, stirring his tea, in which there was no sugar, "how crowded is it, on ahead? How fast would you say you are moving? And where is Dr. Baruch's unit? At Jasina?"

David replied thoughtfully. "The leaders are in

Poland, perhaps at Vijnita; and Dr. Baruch is up with them. I believe that he does not wish to take any more patients, because of the speed at which his hospital must travel; but I do not know very much about such things.

"As for the rest of us," he continued, "there are many thousands on the roads from here to the border. There are great numbers of French and English, Americans, Germans, Hungarians; and armies of ragged saints and beggars. It's like going through the world, to travel twenty miles. The roads are crowded, of course; you can imagine. There's every kind of cart and wagon; but we're making fair time on the whole, perhaps ten miles a day. I'm told that the Jews from Syria and Morocco, are going by ship across the Black Sea to Azov—how many, I don't know. Every day our numbers increase, as refugees come in from Roumania, or Poland. We should gather double our strength once we reach the Ukraine; then we'll be a very long column indeed."

"Double our strength," mused Dr. Kohn. "A few

millions, all told—out of how many?"

"I do not know," said David simply. "So many have died."

Yes, thought Amanda, glancing across the room at her daughter, and catching her breath; and what did you do to save them?

Still—what could they have done? A doctor, and a poet . . .

"Your rich men could have done something," she said bitterly.

David replied quietly: "When the storm broke, everybody thought first of all of himself. There is nothing unusual in that. And besides, what is the difference? Sooner or later we should have had to face it all over again."

Dr. Kohn nodded his head. "Exactly," he exclaimed. "Where there is dislike to begin with . . . But do not let us talk about the past."

And dropping his voice, he said gravely,

"We still have great men among us. Yesterday, Einstein himself went by."

He made a slight, proud gesture with his hands.

"It will be a long time," he said, "before we have hospitals and laboratories again. None of us, I think, will be able to add anything, now, to medicine or to physics, in his own lifetime. But those who come after us . . ." He glanced across the room at the children. "If only they are not too jealous of each other," he added.

David shook his head. "You are asking for the impossible," he declared. "We are a jealous people."

And the two young men smiled at each other, a little sadly.

How strange, thought Amanda, that they should know it.

She looked at David thoughtfully. He was younger than Paul; ten years, perhaps—almost a generation. But what was the good of that? There was no such thing as youth any more among the Jews, no careless and care-free season, given to joy. How could there be? Already their anxieties were too much for them.

However, David at that moment was not in need of pity. Warmed by the tea, he was enjoying himself; for the first time in many weeks, he felt happy, and secure.

He looked, out of the corner of his eye, at Amanda. She sat there, quiet and self-possessed, at home in the world, at home wherever she found herself. That was a strange thing . . . He tried to imagine her childhood in New England, her grave, kind, angular parents, her tall, happy brothers—they had never been unwelcome anywhere, they had never been kept out of anything. Life was their right; it was a simple fact to them, like sunlight, and rain, like trees, and earth.

And for a moment, in the dingy room of the inn, with rain dripping at the windows, she seemed to glow for him with a sort of radiance—the light of life itself as it might be, life as it must be . . . some day . . . for everyone.

"Do you know what I miss, these autumn days?" Dr. Kohn was saying; "I miss the football games; I'd like to kick a football around, again."

To which he added, with shy satisfaction, "I actually got a little tennis, on the way through Austria."

Amanda smiled at him; she might have been a mother, listening to her son just in from school. And David smiled, too; because it made him feel at home, it established something between them.

He wanted her to smile at him, in the same way. But Amanda was looking across the room at her daughter; she had no smile for David. Feeling that he ought never to have expected it, he relapsed into uncomfortable silence.

"Tennis is my favorite game," said the doctor.

"Yes," said David. "Well . . ."

The others rose as he got up to go. "Come again," said Dr. Kohn.

"Yes, do," said Amanda. And she smiled at him after all.

He rode back through the fading twilight. The rain had stopped; and he made his way more easily through the wagons and motors which thronged the roads. The divisions were making camp for the night; on every side were to be heard the sounds of evening, the lowing of cattle, the shrill voices of women, laughter and cries, and the guttural replies of the men. Tents were being erected, wagons driven into the fields, while groups went off to look for water, or fire-wood. The air was cold and wet from the drenching, the clouds rode low above the earth; camp-fires were being lighted, golden and winking in the dim blue air. A chazzan was wailing an old chassidic song as David went by; further on, a man's voice broke into an English tune. There was always the same bustle at the end of day, as family after family left the line, and settled down for the night.

He expected to find his grandmother with Mrs. Blumenthal, in the passes west of Jasina, over which the sky was already darkening. But as he splashed forward on his motorcycle, he saw only Amanda's face before him, as she had looked when she said goodbye.

His heart was filled with it. The right to live, to be

welcome on this earth, to see kindness in the faces about him. . . .

Mrs. Ninian had made her camp in a little wood of pine trees above a stream. Having heated her grandson's soup for him, she was enjoying a game of cards by herself, in the light of the fire which a neighbor had built for her. "Well," she said, not looking up, "did you give him the jelly?"

"Yes, grandmother," said David.

She laid down the king of hearts. "Good," she said. "Poor soul, I hope he enjoys it."

"I think he felt," said David, "that he had a right to it."

"Never mind," declared his grandmother; "he has no family, like you have. Don't be smart, David. If you were sick, you'd want somebody to send you jelly, too.

"As for what he thinks," she added vigorously, "it makes no difference to me one way or the other. Our business is to get to China. Save your arguments until we get there."

And on the king she placed in a firm manner, the queen of spades.

After supper, David went to return the motorcycle to Young Nelson, from whom he had borrowed it. But the prize-fighter was nowhere to be seen; only Manny Jacobs, his manager, sat before the fire, moodily smoking a cigar of the region. "Benny's gone over to see a girl," he announced. "Leave the bike. There's always women in the world. And if it's not them, it's some other trouble."

"Tell him thanks," said David.

So saying, he walked away, to look for Raoul.

He found his friend seated on a fallen tree trunk, at the edge of the firelight. "Ah," said the young Frenchman, as David sat down beside him, "there you are at last. Well—what a day, eh? The rain; what have you been doing?"

To which David replied that he had been to Huste, to see Mr. Alberg at the hospital.

"I took him some jelly from my grandmother," he explained.

"Well, all right," said Raoul; "did you have a

profitable trip?"

David thought of Amanda; in the firelight, his face grew solemn. "Yes," he said; "I did."

Something in his friend's voice caused Raoul to turn toward him. "What is the matter?" he asked anxiously. "You have had an occurrence? You have met someone?"

"Yes," said David quietly.

"There you are," said Raoul. "I cannot let you out of my sight. But all that he says is 'I have been to deliver my grandmother's jelly.'"

"What a sly fellow."

Laying his hand on his friend's shoulder, David shook his head. "Don't be silly," he said; "nothing has happened—I've just met a—friend, that's all; someone I hope, that is—who will be a friend . . ."

"Good," declared Raoul, who was, as a matter of fact, already thinking of something else. "I have quarreled with my father," he said finally.

"No," exclaimed David in surprise.

"It is a fact," said Raoul.

"It appears that he does not wish me to fight."

"Not to fight?" asked David in surprise. "With whom?"

"With anyone," said Raoul.

"But what does he mean?" cried David. "How can we help it?"

The Frenchman shrugged his shoulders. "Exactly," he said. "How can we help it? However, my father says that we are not to fight any more. In agreement with him is Mr. Solomon, the father of the golden-haired Betty. So I replied to him: my Papa, we are attacked, at which we fight, like men of good sense. To which he made answer: I do not wish you to fight, because it makes bad feeling along the way.

"So then I have retired to this tree, to compose my spirits."

David sat staring into the firelight. He was not thinking any longer of battles; he was thinking of Amanda. Somewhere back there in the darkness, she was putting her daughter to bed—talking to her husband, perhaps, or making a last round of the beds in the hospital. He did not ask that she think of him; it was enough to know that she was there.

"Already," said Raoul, "my Leah sleeps in her wagon, between her father and her mother. I have said a prayer for her, but it is in French."

"God will hear it," said David. "He will translate it into Hebrew."

As he spoke, two figures came slowly toward him through the trees—two figures arm in arm, a man and a woman, walking quietly, whispering drowsily.

He thought that he recognized one of them. It was Young Nelson, the prize-fighter. And with him—surely, that slender figure, that golden hair—

He let out a low whistle. Was that what Betty wanted?

All at once he found himself shivering. "I'm cold, Raoul," he said. "Let's go back."

But Raoul was thinking of God, to whom he had, as a matter of fact, addressed a few words. The young Frenchmen looked up into the darkness of the trees, beyond which the night seemed moving with its winds, and with the sound of rain. He closed his eyes, to listen.

"You are right," he said. "God is already speaking."

ALL WEEK the Jews filed through the passes of the
Carpathians, driving their oxen and cattle, their
horses and motors, up the steep roads between forests of spruce and pine, and under thunderous
cliffs. The sun shone now and then; at other times
the rain drenched them; and mountain gales blew
like ice through their sturdy wagon-covers, and
their canvas tents. At the top of the pass there was
snow; the mountains around them were already
white, though for the most part hidden by clouds,
or fog. The air was light and clear, fragrant with
mountain odors, redolent of pine, cold from the
distant snows. The men put their shoulders to the
wheels, shouted and sang; the women sat bundled
in their clothes, or walked beside their wagons,

breathing the fresh, good air; or they huddled under their covers to escape the rain.

The roads were narrow and crowded, sometimes no more than a track; the wheels sank in mud, or jolted over stones. They climbed, winding above the gorges, above forests, and by the side of cataracts whose icy spray blew over them like rain. The great trees, the dark and glistening rocks towered above them as they made their way slowly upward, and toward the east. On those steep and breathless roads, many wagons were lost; and more than one family gazed in horror as its last few belongings rolled like a little avalanche into the chasms below.

The men of Lord Steyne, stationed at crucial points, helped the wagons to round the corners or to cross the ledges, pulled them out of the mud, kept the cattle moving, and herded the children out of harm. As though the pass itself were not sufficiently formidable, its passage was made even more difficult by the fact that the chassidim were celebrating the harvest festival. Singing and dancing, the ragged saints swept up the roads, pushing carts and wagons out of the way, and bruising men and women against the rocks. It was impossible to stop them, for they recognized no authority but God, whom they worshipped at this season with a sort of wild abandon.

Nothing was safe from their mystic fury, nothing was too homely or too sacred for their religious rage. Led by their chazzanim, chanting the traditional songs, they poured upward through the pass in a frenzy of optimism which none of the circumstances of their needy and friendless lives seemed to justify.

They jostled the poor no less than the rich; but even without the chassidim, the pass was full of difficulties for the Hyman Cohens. Madelon felt sick most of the time; and Mr. Cohen was forced to beg a ride for her in a wagon in which there seemed to be some extra room. After that, he pushed his little cart up the steep roads by himself. But he was lonelier than ever; for everybody was too busy to talk to him. So he talked to himself; he imagined that Madelon was there with him. "Just wait," he told her, "until we get over these mountains. A land of honey is what we are coming to. Milk and honey. I will have to get you a new dress, when you begin to get big; but that also can be arranged. We will cross Russia in a sleigh with three horses."

A little later, helping a Galician whose wagon was having trouble in a curve, he said shyly to the wagoner, straining at the wheel, "Perhaps you, also, are a socialist?"

The man looked at him in surprise. Then, straightening up, he tapped his head suggestively. "A lunatic," he said.

"Do not talk—push."

Mr. Cohen pushed. At night he slept with Madelon beneath the same wagon in which she rode during the day. He held her in his arms; and fell asleep without saying anything.

In the morning she was blue with cold; and he begged a cup of tea for her from a neighbor. "My back hurts me," she told him; "it is like a knife. Go, Hyman; leave me here to die."

But the next moment, breathing in the fragrance of the hot tea, she exclaimed,

"If only there were sugar; my stomach is melting for sugar."

And she wept, for sickness, and for all the little homely comforts that were denied her.

The van of the army itself, moving rapidly, had already reached the Polish plains; but the center, in which David and his grandmother had their places, went more slowly. The motor of M. Perez, the banker, ground its way up the mountain a little ahead of the wagon of the Kovnitz Rabbi; and as much again behind Mr. Solomon, who was pressing forward in the company of a group of refugees from Jugoslavia.

Before him, in turn, moved a small flock of sheep from the Hungarian plains.

Mrs. Ninian rode with Mrs. Blumenthal in the latter's carriage. The altitude of the pass was likely to be bad for Mary's heart, and she wanted to be near her. Not that she expected anything to happen; but Mary was old, and one could never tell.

The two ladies found themselves on the afternoon of the fifth day, approaching the top of the pass. Beyond them lay the Polish border, whose guards, in grey uniforms, watched with contempt the endless passage of the Jews past their stations. The sun had broken through the clouds, and the world of mountains lay about them, gleaming in the cold, pure light, lonely and mysterious. The road crossed an upland meadow; on one side the slope rose bare and brown above their heads, while on the other, far below, a slate-cold river dashed itself to foam between the rocks. All about them— save on the road itself—was silence; the lonely peaks, the light and shining sky, blue as a robin's egg; and far off, even to a bird flying, across the endless hills, the distant countries, full of strangers.

"Back there," said Mrs. Blumenthal, nodding her head in the direction from which they had come, "will seem like home to us soon."

Mrs. Ninian touched her friend's hand. "Now Mary," she said, "don't be like that. Look ahead, dear. We'll be in Poland tomorrow."

"Maybe so," replied Mrs. Blumenthal, "or maybe we'll be lying down there, with our necks broke. Don't ask me to look, Frank; it would make me dizzy. The first day, I thought I'd be killed outright, then and there."

"Well," said Mrs. Ninian, "you weren't."

"No, I wasn't," agreed Mrs. Blumenthal. "But now we're even higher up. How are you feeling, Frank?"

Mrs. Ninian sighed. "I have a touch of rheumatism in my legs," she replied, "but I don't pay any attention to it. As I said to David only the other day, I suppose there were old ladies in Egypt. We can't all have it just the way we'd like. Look at that mountain over there, Mary, with the sun on it. That's beautiful; I'd like to live there."

"It's like Mount Marcy at home," said Mrs. Blumenthal. "Though I never saw it in the snow," she added truthfully.

"You're like the little bird that flies backward," said Mrs. Ninian. "He don't want to see where he's going; he wants to see where he's been."

Mrs. Blumenthal smiled. "There is a bird like that," she admitted. "He lives somewhere up in the north." She drew her shawl closer around her, over her coat. "I feel cold," she said. "The sun must be going down."

Mrs. Ninian leaned over and tucked the robe tighter around her friend's knees. Mary had been ailing, she thought, ever since Yom Kippur; ever since they had stood together during the prayer, the Hazkaras Neshomos, the Remembering of the Dead. The solemn Day of Atonement, with its thoughts of the past, celebrated in the sodden fields, in the roadside synagogues; the terrifying sound of the shofar, the sorrowful chanting of the congregations, had done their best to shake a spirit already disposed to falter, had brought the world of the dead too close. She was the one who looked back, she was Lot's wife; the cold of eternity had begun to steal through her veins.

Mrs. Ninian wrapped the robe around her. Her own warmth, she thought, must cheat the cold; her own heart encourage with its steady beat the waning pulses of her friend. "When I get to Russia," she said, "I'm going to buy some postals to send home. And a little silver ikon for Katy Ryan, my old cook. You remember her, Mary, don't you? The one I had for almost twenty years. When I was in Rome, I brought her home a rosary, blessed by the Pope. I wonder would she like an ikon, after all. Well, no matter; I can send her something else."

"Do you remember my Olga?" asked Mrs. Blumenthal. "The one who made such good noodle soup, with matzoth balls? When I had to sell everything, and go away, she brought me all her savings. I didn't take them, but it was very nice of her. Maybe I'll send her a postal, too. But I don't know her address."

"Never mind," said Mrs. Ninian; "you can send it care of my Katy."

Mrs. Blumenthal gazed around her with a pleased expression. "What a light there is on the snows," she remarked. "Like pink icing."

She is feeling better, thought Mrs. Ninian; she speaks of food. I must make her some noodle soup.

And she patted Mrs. Blumenthal's hand.

As they drew near the Polish border, they grew silent and anxious. Suppose they were held up for some reason; suppose they were not allowed to go through with the others. But the Polish soldiers paid no attention to the two old ladies. They had no orders to arrest anyone. The Jews were to go through, and not to stop anywhere, that was all. They hurried them along; and they said to each other that when the last Jew had left Polish soil, then they could count themselves a lucky land.

But to those who were marching, it did not matter in which country they found themselves. Food and shelter were as hard to procure in one as in another; the sun and the rain were the same; and there was no difference in the unfriendly feelings of those whom they met on the way.

They celebrated the Feast of Tabernacles in the passes through which, centuries before, the armies of the Turk had descended into Hungary. Where the horsemen of Solyman had driven their shaggy Asiatic ponies, the ragged chassidim danced for joy, by the roadside, and in the mountain meadows. Pushed to one side, David watched them with wonder, and with a sense of impatience. The harvest festival, he thought. What is there to be thankful for?

But at the same time, he remembered the words: As ye sow, so shall ye reap.

What have we sowed, he wondered.

Troubled in mind, he sought out Raoul. But when he finally caught sight of his friend's dark head, it was bent close to another, over whose coiled brown hair a woolen shawl was tied against the wind. It was Leah, escaped for a moment from her parents; and at the sight of Raoul's face, eager and shining, David drew back. He had no business there; he turned away.

They did not see him. Their fingers were clasped; and they gazed in wonder at the snowy peaks, already blue and cold in the fading light. They said little, for there was little to say; their hearts needed no language. Each was too shy to speak of beauty, too frightened to speak of love.

Raoul was the first to break the silence.

"How good of you to be here with me," he said. "I did not think we would ever meet, and talk together. All day I was walking behind your wagon, at a discreet distance."

"I know," said Leah simply. "I saw you."

And she gave his fingers a light squeeze; after which she wished to let go. But Raoul held her hand tighter than ever.

"You are an angel," he declared. "Where is your Papa?"

Leah looked up and down the road. "He prays," she said uncertainly. "And I am not an angel. Perhaps this is wrong, what I am doing."

"Do not say so," cried Raoul. But Leah shook her head.

"How can you think favorably of one so immodest?" she asked.

"You are more modest than the rose," replied Raoul. "Look—I cannot even see your face. Your shawl . . ."

"The rose is not modest," said Leah seriously.

— 82 —

"You are ashamed of me."

"The lily, then," cried Raoul. "The lily of Sharon."

"It is the rose of Sharon. What ignorance." And she broke all at once into a sweet ripple of laughter.

High overhead the half moon, slowly gathering light, floated above the calm and shining snows. It was not yet night; the lamp of evening still glowed in the sky, and on the slopes above them. Raoul trembled; it seemed to him as if his breath no longer came and went, such was the longing which filled his breast. "Leah," he said, drawing her hand to his face, which was as cold as the wind.

"I love you." And at once he wanted to weep, overcome with relief, with joy, and with pity for himself.

Leah was silent. Her eyes, under the shawl, were quiet, and without light. The shadows of the night rose in silence from the valleys; and she gently withdrew her hand.

"That is wrong," she said. "We are not betrothed. You may not love me."

Folding his arms, to keep from shivering, Raoul gazed at her in an unhappy manner.

"How can you say so?" he demanded.

She did not move. "I am sorry," she said. Her voice little more than a breath, seemed to come from nowhere, or from the moon.

"It is not wrong to love you," he declared. "And in addition I cannot help it. Do you not love me at all?"

She made a little helpless gesture. "You must not ask me," she whispered.

"Do you not love me even a little?"

"It is not proper."

"Nevertheless I am sure that you do."

She sighed; and bent her head. "What must you think of me?" she breathed. "May God, Blessed be He, forgive my rashness."

Silently, in the gathering darkness, while the moon floated above them, their arms went out to each other.

7

DAVID THOUGHT OFTEN in these days of Amanda, and the hospital. He wondered how Dr. Wasserman would manage on the steep and winding roads; and whether the hospital would be troubled by the celebrations of the saints.

But neither his anxious thoughts, nor the songs of the chassidim, penetrated to the passes west of Jasina, where Amanda Kohn was hard at work, preparing her patients for the long journey through the mountains. There was much to do; her husband helped her, and her little daughter also wished to be of assistance.

Ann Kohn believed that she could be of use to her mother, and at the same time enjoy the company of her friend, Alex Wolf. Together they fol-

lowed the doctors about, gazed with silent pleasure
at the sick, and repelled the advances of little Sonia
Walewska, aged seven, who had been brought up
to play the violin. This young prodigy, who was
familiar with the works of Bach and Beethoven, was
unable to understand the repugnance she inspired
in Ann, whose awkward, slender form, and long
curling eyelashes, she admired with all her heart.
However, there was no doubt about it; Ann did not
care for her.

She was too young; she was short, and stocky;
and grown-up people admired her. When Sonia
played on her violin, nobody looked at Ann. And
Ann's little heart, which could love a rabbit, or a
little boy, clenched itself like a fist against Sonia,
whom everyone spoke of with wonder.

"Oh dear," she said; "I wish we didn't have to
play with babies all the time."

Skipping twice, she landed with her long legs
apart, like a frog; after which she favored Sonia
with a look of disdain.

"Yah," said Alex, sawing away at an imaginary fiddle; "all the time playing that old fiddle of hers." As a matter of fact, he did not object to Sonia, himself; but he was loyal to Ann, and he knew what was expected of him.

"That is not the way to play the violin," Sonia told him. "If you would like, I would show you."

Ann made a sound of derision. "Alex is going to learn to play the violin," she chanted.

And addressing the hospital at large, she announced,

"Alex is a baby."

"I am not," said Alex. "Anyhow, I'd rather play the trumpet."

And blowing out his lips, he uttered a loud ta ra.

The German broker, beside whose bed they had stopped for a moment, regarded them with cold blue eyes. "Little swine," he said in his own language, "why do you bother me?"

The two older children, who did not understand him, believed that they were being admired. But

Sonia, who knew better, turned pale.

"Come," she whispered; "let us go away somewhere."

"No," said Ann. "I like it here."

And she smiled at the broker from under her long eyelashes.

"Sonia smells," she announced, to no one in particular.

"Her mama is poor," she explained to the broker. "She never had roller skates to play with, or a doll, or a grocery store . . . or a real fur muff, with fur on it."

It was true; alas, poor Sonia. The nose of the youthful prodigy grew wet, and she rocked unsteadily on her chunky legs. "I don't smell," she said. "Why don't you be nice to me?"

"Because I don't want to," said Ann.

"Look," said Alex; "let's play a game, or something. Let's play what are we going to be."

"All right," said Ann. "I'm first." She thought for a moment; her face took on a dreamy look. "I'm going to be a princess," she announced.

"What are you going to be, Alex?"

"I'm going to be a soldier," said Alex. "I'm going to be a general, and shoot people." He levelled his finger first at Sonia, and then at Ann. "Bang," he said with quiet satisfaction.

"When I get bigger," said Sonia breathlessly, "I'm going to have Menuhin hear me play. My teacher told me so. I'll just go up to him and ask can I play for him. And he'll say yes, and then I'll play." By this time her eyes, too, were moist, as well as her nose; and her lips trembled. "Menuhin," she said bravely. "He'll be nice to me, anyhow."

Her own would understand her. The sturdy spirit faltered before the harsh world of childhood, in which the heart looks in vain for pity, in which the hands are raised always in defense. Overwhelmed with loneliness, and at the limit of her resources, she turned away, and laying her head upon a convenient bed, burst into tears.

"I hate my violin," she sobbed. "I want to have some fun.

"I want a little muff with fur on it, for my hands."

Ann and Alex looked at each other. A faint expression of concern showed for a moment on the boy's dark young face, but Ann's eyes under their long lashes grew hard. "Come on, Alex," she said. "Let's you and me play by ourselves."

She moved away on her long legs, whose awkward knees seemed almost to touch each other.

Sonia raised her head from the bed of Mr. Alberg, where it had been laid, and wiped her eyes with pudgy knuckles. "I guess I'm going home," she said. "Goodbye."

Pale, and weary with pain, Mr. Alberg laid his hand with infinite gentleness on the child's bushy head. "Goodbye, little comrade," he said. "Be glad that you have work to do in the world. And when you are older, play for us the music of the revolution, the music of the poor, whose cares and sorrows are like your own."

"Yes, sir," said Sonia.

THE JEWS CELEBRATED the Christmas holidays and
the Feast of Lights in the valleys beyond the Dnie-
per, between Cherkasi and Byelgorod. They had
been joined by many new units and divisions from
the south, from Africa and Syria, broad-faced Tar-
tars from the Caucasus, swarthy Moors, scholars
from Jerusalem and engineers from Tel-Aviv, ear-
nest and formidable, fighters and planters from
the valleys of Esdraelon and Jezreel, bringing with
them their ploughs, and armed with Arab rifles.
The army lay, swollen to twice its size, along the
roads of the Ukraine, as the leaders strove to bring
about some semblance of order among the many
groups who met as strangers, and in confusion, for
the first time.

Food was more scarce than ever; and there were many more to feed. To make matters worse, bands of ruffians roamed through the woods beyond the lines, beating and robbing those who wandered too far from their wagons. And it was cold; light snow covered the ground, the spoken breath floated like a cloud in the frosty air. Muffled in sheep skins and furs, in blankets, or in the white flowing garments of the south, the Jews huddled before their fires, discussed the meaning of the Law, criticized their leaders, and prepared gifts of the season to exchange with one another.

The Kovnitz Rabbi was holding court in a little hollow, among the trees. Surrounded by learned and pious men, both young and old, he was discussing the Congregation of Israel, which the great teachers of the past had called the Bride of God.

"Israel was created," he declared, "before the world began. 'She is the beloved of God, in which He rejoices.' The Pious Rabbi of Breslau has called her the sister as well as the daughter of the Lord; and the illuminated Zaddik of Korzek says,

'Not even the title of God is denied to Israel, for it is written, I have said, Ye are Gods.' "

"It is true," said an elderly shopkeeper, "that God expressly commanded unto Moses, 'Exalt Israel as much as thou canst, for it is as if thou wert exalting me.' "

"As Eve was sister and wife to Adam," continued the rabbi, "so is Israel wife and sister to the Lord, and to all that pertains to him. Of whom it is said, 'How fair is thy love, my sister, my spouse.' Nothing pertains more surely to the Lord than that which He hath Himself created.

"Everywhere it is the law that man and his wife shall live harmoniously together. For it is said, 'It is better to dwell in the wilderness, than with an angry and contentious woman.' In the heat of fury, words are uttered which can never be forgotten. Anger hurts the heart; in the silence of night, the man remembers, and weeps.

"Now he has quarreled with his sister, Israel; he has driven her forth with angry words. Men will weep for Israel, their spouse; of whom it is said,

'Out of Zion, the perfection of beauty, God shined.' "

"May they weep a long time over me, at home in Kovnitz," said a young tailor.

"That is not at all likely," replied Reb Phineas, the marriage broker; "for inasmuch as they have taken your tailor shop, they will make a profit from your absence."

"Let us not discuss worldly things in front of the rabbi," said the elderly shopkeeper in a humble voice.

"How shall we sing the Lord's song in a strange land?" asked the tailor.

To this the rabbi replied: "Whither shall we go from His spirit? If I take the wings of the morning, and dwell in the uttermost parts of the sea, behold He is there."

"Blessed be He," assented the young tailor; after which he added to Reb Phineas, "Their coats will fall apart in a month, because they do not understand tailoring."

The marriage broker blew on his hands. "My

business, anyhow, goes along with me," he said; with such a meaning glance that the young man began to tremble.

"Hearken and be still," said the shopkeeper, looking timidly at the rabbi, from whom he expected further enlightenment.

But Rabbi Liebkowitz was silent. In the midst of his discourse, he found himself thinking from time to time of his own affairs, and wondering if all was not well in his household. His Leah was too silent, too dreamy for her years; she slept badly at night, she would flush and turn pale by turns; she wept easily, smiled over nothing; and twice within the last week she had used the word Noel instead of Hanukkah, to describe the seasonal holidays. Rabbi Liebkowitz did not know what Noel meant; nor would Leah explain; she merely blushed, and grew more distressed than ever.

Possibly she was ill; but it was not an illness with which the rabbi was familiar. Her nose remained dry, she did not cough; and she was even able to sing.

The Kovnitzer did not wish to discuss with Mrs. Liebkowitz the strange behavior of their daughter. Such a discussion between a rabbi and his wife did not appear to him proper; he would have preferred not to notice anything. However, Mrs. Liebkowitz had other ideas; and on his return she approached him with a grave expression, but in a humble manner.

"It is Leah," she announced, "whose actions give me anxiety."

"Perhaps she is sick," replied the rabbi hopefully. "Such a journey as this, with its hardships, would easily affect the health of a young and delicate maiden."

"She is no more delicate than I am," said Mrs. Liebkowitz, biting her lip. "What it is, is that she sings in the middle of the night, when she thinks I am sleeping. That is not the sort of sickness to which I was accustomed as a young girl. My sickness came in the stomach; my head ached, I turned yellow, and enjoyed fever. I did not wish to sing; everything was gloomy. With Leah, everything is rosy; she is

moist and cool as a cucumber. If I speak to her she
is dreaming; she spills the hot water for the tea; in
a thousand ways she causes me uneasiness."

"A silent and loving woman is a gift from the
Lord," quoted the rabbi under his breath.

Mrs. Liebkowitz heard him. Without learning,
she nevertheless replied from the same teacher,

"Hast thou daughters, guard them."

With these words, uttered in a breathless voice,
she retired in embarrassment to her domestic duties.

Seated at the noonday meal, the rabbi regarded
his daughter with misgiving. The cold, clear air had
caused her cheeks to glow; her eyes sparkled, her
mouth was soft, moist, and red; and she was ap-
parently in the best of spirits. "A sickness?"
thought the rabbi. "My wife is right, she should be
more yellow."

"Come, my daughter," he said to her when the
simple repast was over, "I wish to pay a call upon
the orphans of Yarov, the carter. You will go with
me; and we will talk together about the holidays."

As they moved down the road, between fields

covered with snow, the rabbi asked his daughter questions designed to exhibit her piety, her good sense, and her knowledge of what was expected of a Jewish maiden.

She answered him promptly, and without reserve.

"What is the chief virtue of a maiden?"

"Modesty."

"And what is silence?"

"A jewel beyond price."

The rabbi gazed at the snowy fields, beyond which he could see dark and gloomy forests; and he sighed. "My daughter," he said, "you have caused your mother uneasiness."

"Father, I am sorry. I try in all things to be dutiful."

"It appears," said the rabbi, "that you sing, at night."

Leah grew pale; and remained silent.

"You also spill the hot water for tea."

He gazed at her unhappily. "Perhaps you do not feel well," he remarked.

But Leah seemed to be in perfect health. The rabbi sighed again.

"You will not tell me, my daughter, what is troubling you? I wish to help you; your mother and I are full of sympathy, and concern."

Leah shook her head dumbly; a tear ran down her cheek. "No," cried the rabbi; "it is beyond bearing. She weeps; Leah, my daughter, you are breaking my heart."

Overwhelmed with self-pity and remorse, and against her better judgment, Leah replied in a whisper,

"Perhaps I am in love."

The rabbi stood still; his feet remained rooted in the snow, he gazed at his daughter in bewilderment. "In love?" he said. "What does that mean? How can that be? You are not married. In love? I have not heard you aright."

For answer, Leah gave a small sob.

The rabbi's face grew greyer still. "In love," he said wonderingly, "and without even a husband.

Such a thing has never happened before. And to say it . . . to speak it calmly, so, to the air . . ."

And as Leah made no sign, he added in a small voice,

"Is it possible?"

Presently his face grew dark, and he exclaimed,

"I do not at all understand how this could have happened."

Hearing these words, his daughter burst out weeping.

"Forgive me," she cried, "for I could not help myself."

"Yes," he said, "weep; it will do you good, but it is already too late for weeping. Return now to the wagon; later I shall discuss with your mother what is to be done. But first of all, tell me—who is the man?

"No, no," he cried, before she could answer, "do not tell me—not now, not yet."

And again he added,

"Can such things be?"

Leah returned in disgrace to the camp, where

her red eyes and white cheeks satisfied her mother that something dreadful had happened. But the rabbi remained where he had been standing, lost in grief, in confused and gloomy thoughts. That his daughter, his modest Leah, should say so calmly that she was in love, seemed to him as impossible as though the heavens should fall around him in bits of blue plaster. Even married women did not say such things about their husbands; and for a maiden, whose hair has not yet been cut off, to feel in her bosom, unsanctified by marriage . . .

No, no; there must be some mistake. Perhaps he had not heard aright.

Tomorrow he would go to Reb Phineas, the marriage broker, and ask him if anyone had spoken to him on Leah's behalf. Thereafter he would see . . .

In the meanwhile, Leah must be kept in her wagon. And it would be better, he thought, not to say anything about this to his wife, whose outcries would tell everything to the neighbors.

He walked slowly forward, in the direction, as

he thought, of the Yarov orphans. But he was distressed and confused; and not seeing where he was going, he allowed his feet to follow, without his being aware of it, a small path through the snow which led him finally into the woods. In his dejection, it seemed to him no more than natural that the trees should presently close in on him, and that the light should gradually fail and grow dim; he even felt, in a misty way, that nature shared and sympathized with his sorrow. But when someone caught hold of his beard, he realized that he had gone astray.

He found himself confronted by a number of rough-looking men, dressed in the peasant coats of the region.

"Well," exclaimed one of them, with satisfaction, "here is a Jew. Let us take him to pieces, to see how he is made."

The rabbi's heart stood still for a moment; then he faced his captors bravely. "What do you want?" he said. "Go away; I have nothing for you."

The leader of the band, who had hold of him,

replied: "Jews are wealthy; they have all the money in the world. That is wrong; it is honest men like ourselves who deserve it."

"You are mistaken," said the rabbi calmly. "I have no money. I am not a wealthy man. I am a rabbi, a man of God."

For answer, the Russian struck him over the head, knocking him to the ground. "That is a lie," he said. "All Jews have money. They steal the gold and silver from other people's houses; and hide it in the ground."

So saying, he jumped on his victim, and began to belabor him with his feet. The poor man cried out; he felt his ribs cracking, and he shrieked aloud.

"The Jews," said one of the Russians, who was leaning indolently against a tree, enjoying this scene, "roast little children, and eat them with garlic and onions. This is well known. It is also well known that they do not believe in Christ. They are without Christian love; and so they ought all to be exterminated.

"We are not actually doing anything to you," he

added, as the leader aimed a kick at the rabbi's jaw. "This is simply a little argument between friends, and we do not wish to be criticised for it. If you object, we will do you some serious harm."

"Yes," said another; "it is the Jews who make all the trouble in the world. It is they who make the wars; and who get the money afterwards. Give him one more kick for me, Vassily, before we go back to the village. But see, first of all, if he has not hidden some silver in his pocket, the wicked fellow."

However, at that moment, as the heel of the leader of the Russians was raised above the rabbi's face, they heard a great voice exclaim from behind a tree close at hand,

"The Lord of Israel is One."

A second or two later, the phrase was repeated a short distance away; and again, in fierce tones, at still another point. To this was now added a military command in Hebrew; and a loud sound of crackling wood. Surrounded by avenging troops, and overcome with fright, the Russians ran away as fast as they were able; and a moment later Rabbi Hart stepped out from behind a tree, and helped the disheveled Kovnitzer to his feet.

"Where are the others?" asked Rabbi Liebkowitz, when he had recovered his breath; "the armies who came to assist me?"

"There are no others," replied Dr. Hart. "I am the armies. I remembered Gideon at the well of Harod; and I made myself out to be a host.

"It is a scheme I also used to practise at home, though not in the same way."

"Ak," said Rabbi Liebkowitz, feeling his beard tenderly with his fingers, "what violent men. You have probably saved my life. I am grateful to you; but I did not realize that you spoke Hebrew. I know that you are a rabbi, for you were pointed out to me; but such a rabbi who does not wear a beard . . ."

He stopped long enough to utter a groan. "I cannot move," he said; "my leg is twisted; and I have pains in my back, and in my side. Leave me, my friend, to die; or better, return to the camp, and ask my wife to come to fetch me with a stretcher."

"Nonsense," said the other heartily. "Here—you do not weigh very much. Climb onto my back, and I will carry you home."

And hoisting the Kovnitzer, who protested feebly, onto his shoulder, Dr. Hart started back through the woods.

"Why," asked Rabbi Liebkowitz, between groans, "are all men's hands raised against us? Is it because we are the chosen people; and out of envy? I have a nose, eyes, mouth; I am like anybody else. But I arouse only dislike in the world."

"Chosen?" replied Dr. Hart. "Chosen for what, Rabbi? Perhaps to keep alive in the world the emotion of pity; both in ourselves, and in others."

"Pity is a term belonging only to the Most High," said Rabbi Liebkowitz earnestly. "Among men, there can only be consideration."

"What is the difference?" asked Dr. Hart.

"My learned friend," replied Rabbi Liebkowitz, jolting up and down on the other's back, "there is all the difference in the world. The Law, which is God's

Word, is nothing but the understanding of Man's part, as differing from God's part, upon the earth. Just as there can be no religion without the Law, so there can be no Law without understanding. It is said, 'Let not thine heart be hasty to utter anything before God, for God is in heaven, and thou upon earth.' "

"Ai," he added, as his bearer stumbled over a root.

"Man's part in the world," replied Dr. Hart, "and God's, are the same. They are like father and son in the same vineyard; and among the sons, it is Israel who plays the part of Joseph, who was sold by his brothers into slavery. He is the loving one and the beloved; for he alone has affection, and compassion."

Rabbi Liebkowitz: "Since when has Israel had compassion? That is a word which, like pity, belongs only to God."

Dr. Hart: "Very well—kindness, then. At least, kindness is a Jewish attribute."

Rabbi Liebkowitz: "Go a little more slowly, because I am dying. Kindness . . . where do you look for it? Tell me; and I will go along with you to admire this wonder."

Dr. Hart: "Hold tighter to my neck. For kindness, I look in Jewish hearts. But what I find, often discourages me."

Rabbi Liebkowitz: "Is it not so? Nowhere is kindness, not even in the Jew. Shall I tell you something, Rabbi? Study the Law, not the heart. God gives the Jew the Torah; but he makes his own heart. Ai, what a journey. Why did you not leave me to perish where I was at least comfortable?"

Dr. Hart: "We are almost there. It is true that man makes his own heart; and for that very reason, I like to believe that two thousand years of exile have taught us something. We have had a long and painful lesson; but God must still have faith in us, for the lesson continues."

The Kovnitzer gave a groan. "You talk of too many things," he said, "and in too general a manner. Such talk is not for rabbis, who should concern themselves with the meaning of such terms as pity, and consideration."

"Do you not," asked Dr. Hart, staggering out onto the high-road again, "believe in freedom?"

"Did God believe in freedom?" demanded Rabbi Liebkowitz. "He gave His people the Law. Let them follow it."

And he maintained a dignified silence for the remainder of the journey back to camp. Nor would he speak to his wife and daughter when they came rushing out, white-faced and trembling to receive him.

9

THE LIEBKOWITZ FAMILY took no account of Christmas; for the Kovnitzer, it was the festival of the Maccabees. But to many others from Germany, from England, and from America, the Star, the Three Wise Men, the Angels and the Shepherds seemed more real than the expulsion of the Greeks from Jerusalem. They did not believe in the divinity of Jesus; nevertheless, with enthusiasm and joy they went into the woods to cut down small trees of spruce and balsam, in order to set them up again near their wagons, hung with strings of popcorn, apples, and bits of tinsel.

For many, this alone was the meaning of the season. It reminded them of the past; it was a fairy-tale, in which they lived again the cooky-flavored dreams of their childhood. With infinite faith, in the midst of icy fields, surrounded by sombre forests, they gazed with emotion at the age-old symbols of peace on earth, and good will toward men.

Among them was Amanda Kohn. In the hospital at Cherkasi, composed of an old military barracks, she had set up a tree decorated with strips of silver foil. The kosher butcher turned his face away from it in horror; but the German broker wept openly, because it reminded him of home.

"My mother had each year such a tree," he said, "when we were children in the Fatherland."

And his blue eyes, which gazed upon the world with so much dislike, grew moist with self-pity, and at the memory of his mother.

Paul and Amanda had a tiny tree for Ann, for whom they had also bought a doll, and a little pair of Russian boots. But for each other they had no presents, for they felt that they could not afford anything.

"You've given me too much already, my dear," said Paul; "coming with me, like this."

"Did you think I'd let you go alone?" asked Amanda. "You and Ann? To China?"

And she gave his arm a quick squeeze.

"Great silly," she said.

She was excited, and gay; and for a moment, the Christmas season enchanted her. There had been a heavy fall of snow; the sound of sleigh bells on the roads, the cold winter air, the smell of new-cut balsam and pine, all filled her mind with memories of New England, of Christmas at home, of apples and holly, sermons in church, and visits to the aunts and uncles.

She, too, was having Christmas. There was the tree; and Ann's little boots; and she had even persuaded a peasant woman to part with a roasting goose, in exchange for a necklace of coral, a bright scarf, and her only pair of silk stockings.

"We'll have a real party," she told Paul. "We'll have Alex, and Mr. Wolf; and Dr. Wasserman—we can't very well not; and—do you think?—David Weiss?"

That would be her present to herself. And Paul

was pleased; for he smiled happily. "Good," he said. "And if there's snow enough, I'll get them all to help me build a snow man for the children.

"Only don't give Mr. Wolf too much goose, it won't agree with him."

Now, surrounded by his guests, the doctor sat at table, flushed by a long walk in the fields beyond the town, pressing portions of meat upon everyone. He was not unhappy, except when he stopped to think about it; for he was strong and healthy, and he did not object to hardships. The blood sang with enthusiasm in his veins; he liked the snow, he liked to feel that he was getting the better of difficulties. But when he thought of the future, he grew grave and silent. As for his superior, Dr. Wasserman, he ate without tasting anything; he was grateful that the hospital had got through as far as it had without serious losses; and on Christmas, as on any other day, went over in his mind the amount of adrenaline, aspirin, codeine and iodine which remained.

Mr. Wolf was also in good humor. As he gazed at the small piece of meat which Dr. Kohn had put on his plate, he thought, I have only my life to save, instead of my factory, and my stocks and bonds. They were a great anxiety to me, as I look back on it. But nobody can blame me for losing them.

And he gazed affectionately around him, and at the children, who were laughing because Sonia, the little violinist had been tumbled in the snow and beaten by some Russian children the day before.

Mr. Wolf had been rich; but he did not mind being poor, as long as everybody else was poor. When he got to the Gobi, he would have to begin all over again, because after all, one did not expect to be poor forever. Well, that was all right; it made him feel excited to think that everything lay ahead. As long as it was the same for everyone . . . The world of his anxieties was smaller now; it was curled within his own body, it was not very hard to take care of. His own body, that is, and that of his son. He pushed away his plate with a sigh of regret; he had to be careful of what he ate.

"You are a good cook, Mrs. Kohn," he said.

"There is even a taste of sage in this goose, or maybe I simply imagine it. Do not look surprised; once I could have told you how to cook a goose, myself; and I knew the names and the years of more than fifty wines. My head was full of figures, for I had a wonderful memory. But now I have forgotten everything. I wish that I might have added a bottle of Moselle to the feast; but I no longer have any to offer. I remember a Berncastler Doktor, of 1921; like gold, like heavy gold. But it is just as good this way, for I am convinced that we eat too much.

"As a matter of fact, I hardly miss it any more."

"You look a little thin," said Dr. Wasserman. There was a great deal of pneumonia in the hospital, and no oxygen with which to treat it. He gazed about him anxiously; they must keep their health up, if they could.

Mr. Wolf smiled gently. "I am down to my bones," he replied. "I am dwindled to what belongs to me. No fat, any more, belonging to what I eat, or to sitting all day at a desk.

"Maybe your people have done us a good turn, Mrs. Kohn."

"I'm afraid that wasn't their idea," said Amanda. It chilled her happy mood; and catching sight of David's warm glance across the table, she dropped her eyes, and a faint color spread across her cheeks.

"I have no people any more," she said in a low voice.

And she looked up from under her lashes with a frightened expression.

Led by Mr. Wolf, they sang the old songs together. "Always at Christmas," he said, "my family sang these old songs. Do you remember, Dr. Wasserman, my Uncle Ben? He had no voice for singing; but he was the loudest. That came with the coffee, and after the schnecken, when the ladies had left the room. With the coffee we served a brandy, a cognac of 1878. It was an Otard; or perhaps a Martel. You see, I forget. And then we sang songs."

They joined their voices together, harsh and unmusical, but full of feeling;

"Should old acquaintance be forgot,
And never brought to mind?
Should old acquaintance be forgot,
And days of old lang syne?"

The children sang along, with shrill clear voices out of tune.

After dinner they went to watch Dr. Kohn build a snow man for the children. David stood with Amanda in the frosty air; he was silent, troubled in his thoughts, troubled in his feelings. He had seen her sudden look of being lost; it had entered his breast like the stab of a knife. And in his own unhappiness he tried to comfort her.

"I have thought about you a great deal," he said. "I think that you are very brave."

For a moment he was afraid that he had offended her, for she glanced at him in a startled manner. But her shy laugh reassured him.

"Brave?" she exclaimed. "I? No—it is he who is brave." And she pointed to her husband.

"He does what he must, with so little complaint."

"And you?" asked David.

"I follow my choice," she answered quickly. "There is nothing brave about that."

A grey, leaden sky rolled itself out above them, low over the earth; the air had the smell of snow soon to fall. The square in front of the hospital was deserted; a troika passed in the distance shaking its sound of bells into the weighted air. He tried to forget that he had ever thought her secure in the world. She was alone, a stranger among strangers; it was she, not he, who needed comfort. With a heavy heart, he said: "It is like a dream from which I expect to wake at any moment . . . and do not wake."

She gave him a swift, warm glance out of her brown eyes. "I, too," she said.

He continued more warmly: "But after all, I am glad that the past is over and done with, with all its horrors . . . what lies ahead is new, and fresh; it's like a page with no writing on it."

"Yes," she said in a low voice; "for you. But what is there for me, David?"

He turned to her miserably. "Will you be so

lonely in the new land, Amanda?" he asked. His eyes begged her to say no, begged her to be again the person she had been. But she did not answer; and he thought that her eyes shone with tears. "After all," he said with a sigh, "you were happy where you were. You ought not to have come."

"I know," she whispered. "Perhaps—I ought not to have come."

At that moment, he felt truly lost. But he continued stubbornly.

"So it is you who are brave, after all."

She looked away, into the distance. "What difference does it make to you?" she asked at last, "whether I am brave, or not?"

He wanted to answer: Because there must still be someone in the world for me to run to when I am frightened.

But he could not say it; and soon after moved away, to join Dr. Kohn, who was putting a nose on the snow man.

"How is your grandmother?" asked the doctor. "How old is she—seventy-six? We thought to ask her here today, but at her age, the extra journey . . ."

David replied that his grandmother was well, though suffering, like everybody else, from the dampness and the cold; but that her friend Mrs. Blumenthal was ill. "I doubt if she will get through the winter," he said gravely. "She is quite feeble."

Dr. Kohn would have liked to talk to David, for whom he felt a warm concern; but the children chose this moment to tug at his legs. "Come around this side," cried Alex, "and see what I've done."

"Look what we've done," chanted Ann. "We've made the snow man's botty."

And burying her face in her father's coat, she burst into nervous shouts of laughter.

Like a little bull, or a lover, Alex threw himself upon her, and tumbled her violently into the snow. Then she felt sorry for herself.

"He's hurt me," she shrieked, "Alex hurt me. He's wet my pants. I'm all wet and nasty."

The party broke up then, and David started back

toward Mirgorod. He preferred not to travel after nightfall, for there were many enemies along the roads. He had heard someone speak of wolves, and he knew that the Kovnitz rabbi had been beaten by robbers. One of the Yarov children had been savagely mauled by village dogs . . . He wanted to be brave, but he felt anxious.

How unfriendly the earth seemed to him as he went along through the grey, cold air. The fields lay level on every side; in summer they would be yellow with grain, warm in the sun, heavy with life; but now they were cold and silent, white with winter, save where the fires and camps of the Jews had left dark patches in the snow.

Something had hurt him when he had seen that Amanda was crying. He could not bear to think of her as needing pity; where, then, was he to turn? Around him his people warmed themselves by their fires; soon they would be on the march again, fleeing as before. . . . The road went on and on, they wept and loved, trembled, and died together, each with his private share of loneliness and terror, each with his memory of some land, far away, which he had once called home.

And Amanda at Cherkasi, remembering the loving Christmas of her childhood, the cool and kindly voices, the fresh New England air, remembering her tall and smiling brothers, the warm and friendly houses, the abundance of joy, wept for the world, and for her youth, in a tempest of homesickness.

That night, as the snow fell in the darkness over the level fields, over the dwindling fires and the wagons of the exiles, the body she abandoned to her husband was so tense with anguish, the mouth she pressed to his so salty with despair, that he was frightened for her; and held her in his arms long afterwards, sleepless and shivering, staring into the night, through which the dark and icy winds, full and relentless, carried the snow from village to village, above the shuttered houses, barred to the wind, barred to the wolves, and to the Jews.

In the morning, the snow man stood askew in the hospital yard, a victim of the students and rowdies of the town. He wore a bedraggled caftan, stolen

from an unguarded wagon; and on his sagging chest
hung a sign in Russian:

Here is a miserable Jew. His heart is of ice.
Go further, Jews. Do not stop here.

10

THAT WINTER WAS VERY HARD on the refugees; it was colder than usual, snow fell; and many thousands died of exposure, of wounds, or of disease. Some merely vanished; an entire family, which had fallen behind the march, was said to have been torn to pieces by wolves in the forests of the Don, near Boguchar. Bands of roving peasants hung upon the edges of the march, ready to beat and rob the stragglers even of their insufficient rags; the only hope of the exiles lay in keeping together, as near their own soldiers as they could; and of sharing the food and the shelter which their leaders procured for them by one means or another.

Ill from the cold, thin with hunger, their feet often wrapped in burlap, they plodded on through

the mud and the snow, among the motors and wagons. But fuel was scarce, and some of the motors
had to be abandoned. Their owners walked, or were
taken into the wagons of relations, and acquaintances. Many friendships were begun in this way on
the road from Byelgorod to Kamishin. The aged
found ready hands to help them; and children such
as the Yarov orphans were cared for by the women,
whose hearts, in the midst of their own distress, still
beat with charity and pity.

However, not all the Jews were equally penniless;
and those with money were able to buy themselves
furs and boots and other articles in the markets as
they went along. Mr. Nieman wished to tax these pur-
chases, in order to procure food for those without
means, and supplies for the hospitals. However, this
proposal aroused great uneasiness among the rich,
who were afraid that they might lose their possessions.

They clung to what they had, although they no
longer had very much. But the communists wanted
to take that also away from them. And Mr. Alberg

did not hesitate to call the socialists cowards and traitors, because they would not join the communists in seeking to achieve this end.

The divisions which had come from the north, from Galicia, from Lithuania, and Latvia, were vexed because they were being led to Mongolia, instead of to Palestine.

"Lead us to Jerusalem," they cried; "what is this nonsense about the Gobi Desert?"

For they would not believe that Jerusalem had been taken away from them again. They believed that in the end they would find themselves in Zion.

And the Zaddik of Povsk, a leader of the chassidim, explained,

"The trouble with Mr. Nieman is that he is not a Jew."

But Hyman Cohen among others, did not believe this nonsense. He said to his wife Madelon: "Mr. Nieman is as much a Jew as anybody. It is only that people want to make trouble. What I say is, let us all be friendly, and do things in a nice way."

Thus he expressed his opinion of the communists, who were forever fighting and getting killed.

Mrs. Cohen sighed. The battles of the liberals and the orthodox, the communists and the socialists, were matters of indifference to her. The life she was carrying absorbed her body, gaunt with hunger, racked with cold and with fatigue; and filled her mind, already lonely and afraid, with new and daily terrors. She tried to remind herself of the pioneers, of the intrepid women who had ridden the great wagons westward across America; but these were feeble fancies, compared to her own overwhelming longings. She thought of the little delicatessen store at home, with its glass counter, piled with food, its smell of pickles and limes, of sausage and cheese. . . . She wanted fresh fruit to eat, warm water to wash with, a soft bed to lie in; she wanted new clothes, a coat to cover her awkward figure; she wanted to see flowers again, and grass. Her spirit cried out for warmth; the endless cold numbed her body, already too heavy for her legs to carry; the snowy fields hurt her eyes, too often filled with tears. And the winter sky, sometimes so sharp and blue, sometimes misty, like milk, pressed upon her heart. She thought that her child would die of the weight of it.

"Will there ever be green grass again, Hyman?" she asked. "Or does the winter go on forever in this country? Better they should kill me, and be done with it; because I cannot bear it any longer."

But Hyman, his pale blue eyes watery with cold and with anxiety, pressed her wasted hand beseechingly between his own. "Now, now," he cried, "now, now—who talks of winter going on forever? Grass and flowers are waiting for us—just a little ways ahead. You will see. And new clothes, a new dress —everything. Leave it all to Mr. Nieman; he knows what he is doing."

As a matter of fact, the aged leader did not spare himself in caring for the people who blamed him for everything. He appeared along the line of march at all hours, and in all places, asking funds of the rich, conferring with men of importance; or tasting the stew or the gruel in the humble kettles of the poor. Where it was possible to help, he helped; but he was not afraid to scold where it was necessary. With him went Steyne, his grey eyes quiet and alert above his close-cropped moustache; and Rabbi Hart, deep-voiced and leonine, anathema to the orthodox, but a great power in dealing with the police and the officials of the region.

When they had passed down the entire line of march, they returned to their positions in the van, in order to prepare the way, to choose the best road, and to purchase supplies. The villagers turned out at first to watch the exiles go by; but after a day or two, they put up the shutters of their houses, and remained indoors, hostile and embarrassed because there were so many more Jews in the world than they had imagined.

Mr. Alberg would have liked to fraternize with these people, who lived under the red banner of the proletarian state. But the collectives had not taught them to be trustful of strangers. And when he took the opportunity to make several speeches in Yiddish, in praise of the soviets, he was soundly beaten by the inhabitants of Rossosh and Boguchar.

During those bitter days, in the snow, the rain, and the freezing winds, the Jews did not want for music. But those who sang were the cantors, or mothers to their babies; and the songs which they sang were traditional and religious. The young no longer danced; and the great violinists let their fingers grow stiff, while the strings of their fiddles snapped of cold in their cases.

The scientists, on the other hand, disputed as warmly as ever the questions of biology, physics, chemistry, and mathematics. But they could not be sure of anything, due to the absence of laboratories, and other equipment. The thesis of Professor Eischenheim, once of Leipsig, concerning the cell, which he had been attempting to prove by means of scorpions, seemed to Professor Ludwig Baumann, of the Kaiser Wilhelm Institute in Berlin, more fraught with peril than any of the hardships or dangers he had been obliged to face since he had escaped from Germany.

Glowing with indignation and anxiety, he begged

his friend, Gottfried Kamp, once director of the Düsseldorf orchestra, to accompany him on an expedition to the rear, in order to discuss with Dr. Wasserman in his hospital certain practical and experimental aspects of this theory.

They set off early in the morning, moving counter to the tide of men and wagons rolling to the east. The air was bright, the professor's cheeks were red and windbitten; the sun shone down, his boots scuffed up a little storm of newly fallen snow with every step. He paid no attention to the hordes moving past; his slight, erect figure, followed by the tall music master, butted its way westward, in the direction of the primitive laboratories of Dr. Wasserman.

"These young men," he said, "get in their heads an idea, and then all nature must agree with them. But one cannot allow a mere supposition to cloud the objective point of view. Is it not so? My dear Kamp, what do you think; shall we walk a little to the side of the road, to be away from these cows which are coming? Are they, indeed, cows? Is it possible that we are taking with us to the Gobi Desert, cows? What an excellent idea. I should never have thought of it; but there they are. Well, where we are going, Dr. Eischenheim will find plenty of animals to help him with his never-seriously-to-be-entertained experiments."

Herr Capellmeister Gottfried Kamp walked along without noticing anything. The great works of the masters sang themselves over and over again in his mind, while he conducted in imagination the horns and fiddles of the Düsseldorf Philharmonik. But he was unhappy, for many of the masters whom he revered had hated the Jews. He was an admirer of Wagner and Richard Strauss; and now he was obliged to keep his mind on Goldmark and Mendelssohn; when he hummed Brahms to himself, it was with an air of apology.

Still, perhaps Brahms would not mind, after all, if a Jew admired him.

Of course, art should be above such things; but there was no question about it, there was difficulty in enjoying to the full the good things of earth, when they were the work of the so-bitter enemies. One wanted to; but one felt in some way embarrassed.

They were still some four miles from the hospital when he became aware of a little girl trudging silently along beside him. For a while he paid no attention to her, his mind being taken up with the part of the second flute in the third Leonore. But after she had twice fallen in the snow between his feet, he stooped, and picked her up. "What do you want, little girl?" he asked in German.

Sonia Walewska, for it was she, looked sturdily up at him. "Nothing," she said. "I don't want anything."

"Hm," said Herr Kamp. "Then why do you fall between my feet? You know, perhaps, who I am?"

"Yes I do," said Sonia. "I go to concerts."

Herr Kamp was pleased. "Ah," he said. "So you go to concerts. That is very good. And you remember me. Excellent. Perhaps you can recall something that we played. It cannot, at least, have been very long ago."

"I know what you played," said Sonia. "You

played the Brahms, with Adamowski. He played it very bad; his intonation was very bad. It was one of his bad days."

Kerr Kamp smiled down at the little figure, whose head barely reached to his knee. "So," he said; "you are a musician. And you play the fiddle, too?"

"Yes I do, " said Sonia.

"Good," said the capellmeister. "You play little pieces no bigger than yourself."

"I play the Brahms," said Sonia. And she added truthfully, "I can't reach all of it. I'm too little."

Herr Kamp gave Sonia a look of surprise. "So small," he said. "And yet she plays the Brahms."

"Some day I'm going to play for Menuhin," she told him. "My teacher promised me."

"You shall indeed," said Herr Kamp. "You shall indeed. And for me, too. We will do the Brahms . . . well, no, we will do the Mendelssohn together. When I have found a piano again. Such little fingers; my goodness. Will you play for me, little miss, and for my friend, the Herr Professor?"

"Yes I will," said Sonia.

And because she was looking up at him, she fell down in the snow again.

Professor Baumann, who had hurried on ahead, was waiting for the capellmeister to catch up with him. "My dear Kamp," he said, "is this the time to talk to children? Go, little girl, go, little one; we still have a long way to walk."

"This is a musician, Baumann," said Herr Kamp, brushing the snow from Sonia's jacket; "a violinist, a prodigy. We have been discussing music; soon she will play for us, a concerto by Mendelssohn. She speaks of Adamowski as though he were a student. . . . That is genius, my friend, to be so young, and already to speak of the masters with impatience."

"That is not genius," replied the professor, "that is youth. It takes for itself always the prerogative of impudence. It is the same in science. A young man discovers that in the scorpion it is possible to find an egg in which the cell will show, or will not show. . . ."

"Yes, yes," broke in Herr Kamp; "you are talking of Eischenheim. He is already a man of fifty. But we are talking about music; and this little lady is perhaps not yet eight years old."

"I'm seven," said Sonia. "Going on eight."

"There, you see," said Herr Kamp, "she is seven, going on eight. To the musician there is no such a thing as age. Music is such a language for the whole world; it is open to everyone."

But at once he grew silent, remembering that he was no longer able to play the works of Richard Strauss with the same joy as formerly.

"Well," said Professor Baumann, "all right; but do not let us stand here and argue, when we have still so far to go."

So saying he strode away, without waiting for the capellmeister.

"Goodbye," said Herr Kamp to Sonia. "Auf wiedersehen."

"Goodbye," said Sonia. And as his long figure, bent over the professor in argument, moved down the road, she called after him,

"Auf wiedersehen."

11

THE REFUGEES WERE ENCAMPED in the forest, under the great boughs weighted with snow. Their voices echoed and re-echoed among the trees, from which came a sound of chopping, as men set about furnishing their wagons with piles of logs. Now, of an evening, the camp fires drew together as close as possible, while stories were told of the gloomy forests in which were to be found robbers, wild animals, and evil spirits.

During the day, the Jews threaded their way eastward among the trees. They spoke little, and hurried onward, anxious to get out of the forest as quickly as possible. A mysterious and brooding silence enveloped the earth, under the heavy boughs from which fell dark shadows and little clumps of snow. In the evening, as the light began to fade, they made camp; the men went off with axes and saws, and the fires were lighted behind them in the dusk.

David went out with the others, to cut wood for Mrs. Ninian's little stove. His wind bitten face glowed as he worked, his hands were firmly gripped, and his axe made a musical sound against the trees. At such moments as this, before he was too tired, and while the blood ran strongly in his veins, he felt free and strong, and the tragic journey no longer frightened, or even troubled him. It seemed to him that he no longer depended upon others to save him; with each blow of his axe, he imagined that he was saving himself.

At the same time, he realized that when the glow had gone out of his blood, he would feel less happy and hopeful. And swinging his axe in a wide circle, he remarked to the man next to him, who was also gathering wood,

"Let us hope that this clear weather holds a little longer."

The man made no reply, and David stopped to look at him. He saw that he was little more than a boy, and that he was shivering under his thread-bare coat. He had no axe; he was looking for dead branches, not too thick, to break with his hands.

David addressed him in halting Yiddish. "You are a Pole?" he asked.

"No. I am a Lithuanian."

And the young man went on with his work, without saying anything more.

David returned to his chopping. But he no longer felt comfortable in what he was doing. He heard the ring of axes in the forest, the sound of men calling to one another; he heard, farther away, the lighter voices of the women about the fires; they drew him back against his will, they separated him from the little world of himself in which he had been happy, they called him to return. . . . He was no longer a man alone, depending only upon himself; the voices drew him back to the fear and the cold, to the losses and the griefs of others, to strangers whose lives were mixed and mingled with his own, whose fate, whose destiny was his. It isn't just me, he thought; it's all of us . . . cutting wood here, side by side . . .

In the forest, night was already falling, darkness was already walking among the trees. A profound sadness overwhelmed him; his own body seemed to take on the cold and the hunger of his companions. And in his mind, he said to the young man beside him, "I can't very well let you freeze. We have to get to China together. Otherwise what is the use of all this?"

And without thinking any more about it, he dropped his axe, and picking up his sweater, placed it around the youth's shoulders.

"There," he said. "Now it's up to you to manage somehow."

The young man stared at him in surprise. "Well," he said finally, in his own language, "that's all right." He thought that David was rich; and he did not know whether to be grateful or not.

Blowing on his hands, David gathered up his logs and returned to his grandmother's wagon. He moved with difficulty in the darkness, and his thoughts, also, were uneven and confused. He did not regret the loss of his sweater; he was sad because, for a little while in the forest, he had felt happy and alone, a man by himself, with his own wood to gather, and his own hunger to appease; and because thereafter he had been drawn back into the world of his exile again, obliged to take up his share in all those other lives, with their burden of conflict and dread. It isn't hard to give away a sweater, he thought; what is hard is not to give away at the same time the sense of one's own private and personal destiny. To be cold and hungry because others are cold and hungry, is easy; what is hard, is to remember that there are other things, too, in the world, besides hunger and cold. To walk side by side with the lowly, yet not to feel lowly, to live with the poor in spirit, yet not to be poor in spirit, too. . . .

That is what is hard.

12

MRS. BLUMENTHAL WAS DYING. The little bird that flies backward was approaching the last dark land, her eyes still gazing hungrily at where she had been. The mists of distance, mellow and golden, surrounded those shores whose contours were no longer visible. Stretched on a wooden cot in a covered wagon, the dying woman relived the grateful hours of her youth, and in those mildly glowing memories, forgot the cold which crept in through the canvas sides of the wagon, stuffed with felt to keep out the wind.

The few members of her family who still remained, were busy elsewhere; but they came to take leave of their relative, to say farewell in low voices, heavy with weariness and with anxiety for themselves. They knew that there was nothing they could do; and in addition, the fate of their own children weighed heavily on their minds.

But Mrs. Liebkowitz, the rabbi's wife, came often to the wagon, the august presence of death giving her the courage to intrude on so elderly and so foreign a lady. With Mrs. Ninian she took turns watching at the bedside, striving with her humble smile and willing heart, to make up for the fact that she did not understand what Mrs. Blumenthal said to her. It was Mrs. Liebkowitz who supplied Mrs. Ninian with matzoth for soup; too late to nourish, it nevertheless brought a smile to the dying woman's face. "That's good," she said; "that tastes good, Frank. It's like my Olga used to make."

"The noodles aren't much," said Mrs. Ninian gruffly; "and there's no parsley. But no matter, Mary; we'll have parsley next time."

"Next time," whispered Mrs. Blumenthal, and patted Mrs. Ninian's hand. "Yes—that's it.

"But you'll eat it alone, my dear."

She knew that the end was not far off; and since

there was no help for it, she awaited it without fear. She was not unhappy, for it seemed to her that her pain was already over and done with. Instead of the bare fields, with their white patches of snow, she beheld again the daisy meadows of her youth; she saw again the young girl she had been, and watched with eyes filled with understanding, the panorama of her life. That is the way it was, from the beginning to the end; she needn't worry any more, it was finished, it was whole.

She had a few possessions to leave, warm clothes to give to the poor, an old brooch for Mrs. Ninian, a paisley shawl for Mrs. Liebkowitz. "You give it to her, Frank," she said. "She's kind, though she don't understand me. It's nice to make friends, the last thing you do."

"Don't talk like that," said Mrs. Ninian.

Mrs. Blumenthal smiled weakly. "You don't have to fool me," she whispered. "I know I'm going; and I don't care. I thought maybe I'd be afraid to be left behind; but it don't matter."

Her dim eyes clouded; and her mouth trembled.

"There's so many of us staying behind," she said bravely.

"Do you believe in God, Frank?" she asked at length.

"Yes, Mary," said Mrs. Ninian, firmly. "I do."

"So do I," said Mrs. Blumenthal. "And He won't leave me all alone. Do you remember when we were children how we used to go to the zoo; and how we worried for fear father would lose us, that we'd be left behind . . . but he never did. I keep thinking of that, Frank; he never did."

"Rest a little," said Mrs. Ninian; "you'll tire yourself out."

"Do you remember my wedding?" asked Mrs. Blumenthal. Her voice was light as breath; and she spoke with difficulty. "It was in the spring, and the house was full of lilies of the valley. My Leon was as white as the flowers, as he stood beside me under the canopy. Afterwards we went to Niagara Falls, and soon the children began to come; not many, for those days, and they're all gone, now. But I was blessed with happiness.

"So maybe we'll meet again, my Leon and I."

It was a way of saying that she believed in God, it was an expression of faith. For she did not really expect to see her husband again; she did not even remember him very well. But she believed that her joys and her sorrows were not without meaning, that they were part of a plan whose design escaped her. The bones of her people were laid in so many corners of the earth, the dust of her ancestors was strewn along so many roads. . . . Was it all for nothing? Surely, surely, her father knew best; he would take her where she was going.

Raising herself on her elbow, she said in firm tones:

"I'll never believe it was all for nothing, Frank."

She said little more, except to beg a sign of some sort above her grave, in case anyone ever wanted to know where it was. She hated to be lost. Perhaps death would be less lonely, if she knew where she lay. But even that anxiety faded in time, as she sank deeper and deeper into the mists which rose about her, filled with the echoes of the past. And when, a little while later, she closed her eyes for the last time, the voices she heard dimly around her seemed to be those of her friends; she thought it was her mother who told her goodnight.

Like a child she turned on her side, and fell asleep in the wide plains of Russia, near the little town of Veshenskaya, between the Volga and the Don.

Mme. Perez received Mrs. Ninian in her arms as she stumbled stiffly away from the bed. Wrapped in dark furs which accentuated the pallor and the withdrawn expression of her face, the wife of the banker supported the weary old lady across the uneven ground toward her own wagon. Mrs. Liebkowitz came hurrying to help her. "She is worn out," said Mme. Perez, "the poor old lady. But what courage."

And as she patted Mrs. Ninian's hand, she smiled at the rabbi's wife, for the first time, and in a shy and friendly way.

The death of Mrs. Blumenthal, whom she had seen so often in the company of Mrs. Ninian, touched her; it was like the death of people at home, in France—quiet, natural, from old age, and without violence. It made the two old ladies seem real to her. This one who was left had had a friend, there had been two of them; and now there was only one. That was something which happened to old ladies everywhere.

The little boudoir on the Avenue Friedland no longer occupied her thoughts; instead, she saw about her in the fields and woods, the pale companions of her exile, as homeless and friendless as herself. She was not proof against emotion; she, too, could feel . . .

"Come," she said gently to Mrs. Ninian, "let me pour out for you a little cognac; it will do you good.

"You come, too," she said to Mrs. Liebkowitz.

Mrs. Ninian went with her, without caring. Her mind was empty; she felt, rather than thought, It is over; Mary is gone.

And she wept quietly, not so much for sorrow, as out of pity for her friend, whom she was obliged to leave behind, alone, under the snow.

It's not as though she liked being alone, she thought.

"I will come often to see you," said Mme. Perez, "if you will permit."

"I don't know what you're saying," replied Mrs. Ninian, "but no matter."

She felt very tired; she would have liked to join Mary, to fall asleep, too, not to wake any more. Before her and behind her lay the icy road; nowhere was there rest and warmth. Only Mary was at home; only Mary had no further to go.

"I don't know what's the matter with me," she said apologetically to the two women who were helping her across the uneven ground. "I don't feel very good. I guess maybe I'm tired . . . I feel the cold more than I used to. Mary never liked the cold. But at the end she didn't seem to feel it any more."

She stood still, and gripped Mme. Perez by the arm. "Do you think the ground is frozen, under the snow?" she asked faintly.

Mme. Perez was sympathetic, but she did not understand English. She replied not irrelevantly in her own language, "The good God will cause you to forget your grief in the spring, in the new land."

And Mrs. Liebkowitz smiled at her gently, drawing the shawl closer around her trembling shoulders.

Mrs. Blumenthal was buried the following day, in a field at the foot of a little hill covered with dark pines. The air was bright and frosty, the sky was the milky blue of winter, paling away to the color of light at the horizon. On the road beyond the field, the Jews moved slowly past; they paid no attention to the little party, or to the scene with which they were all too familiar. They flowed by like a river, men, wagons, and animals; and the sound of wheels and voices, of cries and commands, came distantly across the snowy field, like the murmur of a stream. The road led eastward; beyond them, and all about, the land lay quiet and bare, cold and serene and still. The sky seemed full of peace, the very soul of quiet hung above the fields.

Mrs. Ninian, wearing an old black veil, stood at one side of the shallow grave, between David and

Mme. Perez; and Mrs. Blumenthal's few relatives
at the other. Rabbi Hart had come back from
Veshenskaya, to read the burial service; and as the
rude coffin was lowered into the ground, he recited,
in his deep voice, the age-old words:

"The Lord is my shepherd, I shall not want. He
maketh me to lie down in green pastures, he leadeth
me beside still waters. He restoreth my soul, he
leadeth me in the paths of righteousness for his
name's sake.

"Yea, though I walk through the valley of the
shadow of death, I will fear no evil; for thou art
with me, thy rod and thy staff they comfort me."

He spread out his hands, above the grave. "The
Lord giveth," he said, "and the Lord taketh away.
Blessed be the name of the Lord."

Then he addressed the dead woman.

"My daughter, be not afraid of death, thy cove-
nant. Remember that those who went before, and
those which come after, will be with thee. Thy sisters
sleep beside thee in the wilderness; Zipporah and
Ruth, Miriam and Deborah. Dream with them of

Zion, of a peaceful land and a happy people."

And as the coffin was covered with earth and snow, he added tenderly,

"Sleep well, sister and mother; and do not think that we will forget you. We leave you with those who slumber, whose work is done, whose journey is ended."

And David, feeling his grandmother's hand trembling on his arm, thought to himself: we are one people, although we are of many minds, and our opinions divide us. But those who slumber are not divided; they are one. They belong to history, they are the true Jews. They are the men of Joshua and David, of the second Temple, and the wars of Rome. The streets of Lisbon saw them die; their ships crossed the seas, to the new world. They have given us our history, chapter by chapter. You who sleep, as they sleep, you will not wake again in this world full of pain and confusion. If you wake at all, it will be in some gentle heaven, with the ladies of Aragon and Castile.

Mrs. Ninian stood for a moment looking down at

the grave. She said nothing; her eyes were wet, and she made a little gesture, as though to throw a flower down on it. But her hands were empty.

With bent head, she turned, and walked away.

13

DAVID SAW AMANDA AGAIN; they walked together by the banks of the Volga, near Kamishin. The winter was nearly over, and the weather was more moderate, although patches of snow were still to be seen in the shadowy parts of the fields, and under the trees. They had much to talk about, and many questions to ask; they found each other thin, and worn-looking.

Amanda wanted to know how Mrs. Ninian had survived the loss of her friend. "She is not unhappy," David told her; "she is like a child who forgets. . . . But we're all like that, Amanda. There's so much to do; and each day's march makes its own demands. Life is to be lived, on this jour-

— 154 —

ney—even for an old lady. There's no time to think of death.

"But tell me about yourself. I've thought of you so much."

It was not strictly true; although at the moment, David believed it. And Amanda who wanted—and yet did not want it to be true, grew faintly rosy with pleasure. "I've been busy," she said. "There's been so much to do in the hospital. And we have had little Alex Wolf to live with us."

"Then his father . . . .?" asked David.

She nodded briefly. "His heart failed him very suddenly," she said. "But Alex is no trouble, poor lamb."

"And Ann?" asked David.

"She's well, thank goodness."

And she added suddenly,

"I have thought of you, too, David."

It was true; since that day when they had stood together in the snow, she had thought about him a great deal. He had pitied her, and that had made her

— 155 —

unhappy. She wanted to get something straightened out between them.

But she did not know how to begin. She looked at him out of the corner of her eye; yes, he had changed, he was thinner, and older—harder, and more direct, she thought—even happier than he had been. She knew that he had not missed her; and her heart sank.

"Well . . ." said David.

He, too, felt a little uncomfortable, and did not know just what to say. For he was no longer the same as he had been at Huste, or Cherkasi; the long winter march had left its mark on him. It had wasted his body; but it had toughened his spirit. He was no longer anxious, or resentful, or uncertain. Day after day the army had toiled eastward across the plains, and he with it; they had crossed rivers and frozen streams, they had passed through forests whose dark branches, weighted with snow, had made a roof above their heads. He had been with his people. . . . He had hunted hares with some, he had broken bread with others; he had watched through the night with shivering men, hearing in the darkness the distant baying of dogs, or wolves, he did not know which. . . . They had been cold and hungry together, they had sat around the same fires, they had joined their voices in the same prayers, and in endless discussions. He no longer felt alone among the Jews.

He tried to tell Amanda what had happened to him.

"After a while," he said, "people lose their shyness and their dread of one another."

But Amanda shook her head. "I'll never feel at home among your people," she said. "Never."

"I don't know," replied David soberly; "I'm not so sure.

"I wonder," he said after a while, "if we Jews are so different from other people. We don't in the least resemble one another. I mean—I'm much more like you, Amanda, than like Reb Phineas, the marriage broker. No one would take me for a Galician, or a Levantine. And look at Raoul—no one was ever more French than he. There's no such thing as a Jew,

Amanda; there are only Jews. Paul, and I—and little Alex Wolf . . . of course, we're not like your own family. But are we so different?"

She smiled at his earnestness, which she knew was for her sake, not his. "No, David," she said.

"Perhaps," he went on, "when we've lived for a while in the new land, we'll be able to say that a man is a Jew, without having to say that he's a German Jew, or a Spanish Jew, or a Russian."

"Perhaps," said Amanda, "he'll be a Mongolian."

"That is possible, too," said David soberly.

They walked slowly along the broad, low bank of the great river, which, dark with cold, flowed southward toward its many deltas. Flat barges were ferrying the travellers across the stream; a river steamer from Astrakhan puffed its way northward, against the tide, bound for Pokrovsk, and the ancient Ekaterinenstad. While they waited for the ferries which were to take them to the opposite shore, the Jews rested along the sandy river-bank, watered their cattle, or threw into the stream improvised fishing lines baited with pieces of meat. They were the rearguard of the army; most of the divisions were already across, on their way to the great steppes, to the lakes and mountains south of Orienburg. For this reason only a few Russians, mostly women and children, remained to gaze at them with curiosity in which there was no trace of friendliness.

The air was damp, a light mist rose from the water. Sweet woodsmoke drifted in the breeze, along with the odors of cattle, and the smell of the river, of wet sand and weeds, and watersoaked logs. David and Amanda sat together on an upturned river skiff, gazing across the dark and smoothly-flowing stream to the opposite shore, whose wooded cliffs, blue and misty in the distance, seemed to speak of plains and mountains still to be crossed, of dangers and difficulties still to be overcome.

"David," said Amanda suddenly, "do you still think me brave?"

And she gave a dry swallow in her throat, waiting for his answer.

"Yes," he said after a moment. "But it doesn't surprise me any more. Even Jews are brave, Amanda . . . sometimes . . . and in their own way. They're not very dashing, perhaps; but they have fortitude. What other race or people could have stood as much?"

He put out his hand; and she placed her own, thin and cold, within it. "The further I go," she said, "the more frightened I get.

"No—" she said, as he started to reply—"don't speak. Don't tell me that you're sorry for me; I can't bear it. That was what made all the trouble . . . I wasn't sorry for myself, or frightened, before. But ever since Christmas . . . We seem to be so far from home. And we go on, and on."

"I know," he said gravely; "one doesn't expect the world to be so wide."

How strange, he thought, that I should be comforting Amanda. But it no longer makes me unhappy. That, too, is because I look forward, and do not look back any more.

"I hate myself like this," she said.

He answered thoughtfully: "See . . . we sit here, you and I; and we are happy together, we talk, we understand each other—better, even, than Dr. Hart and the Kovnitz Rabbi—here, on this earth, which we share, beside this river whose water flows by us both. We are friends, we love each other as friends should . . . and all about us are others who would love us, too, if we would love them. They are hard to find, because they are shy, or fierce; and they do not look very appetizing. But they ask very little, Amanda; though perhaps when we get to China, they will try to get more for themselves."

She moved closer to him on the upturned skiff; she felt peaceful, and quiet. It was strange, this shift-about of their relations, but she was glad of it. She had never wanted David to turn to her for security; her own husband, whom she loved, had never asked it of her. Nor had he, in turn, been able to help her; from his forthright and energetic spirit, so much like her own, she drew no comfort. He did not feel lost, and so he could not be expected to find himself again. But she, the stranger among them, the alien among the exiles, had been lost indeed; and she could follow David with a thankful heart, as he made his way home.

"As you say," she remarked, "we are not unalike, David. I'm sure that some of these people are as strange to you as they are to me. Do you think they'll ever like me? Not really be fond of me, perhaps— but just feel friendly toward me? Because, if not . . ." Her voice wavered, and she drew her breath sharply.

They sat close to each other, their shoulders touching, gazing together, with unseeing eyes, at the sombre river. A gentle current of peace ran through them, their hearts were linked together, they felt like brother and sister. He put his arm around her, and she let her head rest on his shoulder. "Do you, David?" she said.

In that question, he knew that she asked him many things. Moved, and happy, and in a peaceful voice, he replied:

"I love you very much, Amanda."

"I'm glad," she said. It was what she wanted; and

she knew what he meant. "I like you, too," she murmured.

He pressed her gently to him. "Now tell me about Paul," he said, "and Ann. And about Mr. Wolf, who died, and little Alex . . ."

"Yes," she said obediently. "Well . . ."

After a while they arose, and returned hand in hand to David's wagon. There they found Mrs. Ninian, who had been looking for her grandson. "David," she said; "there you are; we're about ready to cross."

And shaking hands with Amanda, she added,

"I'm glad to meet you, my dear. David has spoken of you so often."

"Thank you," said Amanda happily.

Mrs. Ninian looked at the young woman's tired, peaked face, with its gentleness all for her grandson. "I think there's time for tea before they call for us," she said. "Come in and warm yourself. I'd like a cup myself, with all that water to cross."

They sat about the little stove in the wagon, while Amanda told Mrs. Ninian about the hospital. "We shall stay here at Kamishin for a few days," she said, "to take on supplies, and to rest. I'm afraid that the hardest part of the journey lies ahead of us, across the steppes . . . I don't know when I shall see you again, David."

Her brown eyes, dark with dread, looked sadly into his; she pressed his hand under cover of the little table.

"Until the spring, Amanda," he said gently.

He, too, felt suddenly lonely; his brave mood wavered, he bit his lip. After all, the spring was far away. "I shall miss you," he said in a low voice.

"Until the spring," she echoed. "We can go on till then." And she raised the cup of bitter tea to her mouth, as though it were a pledge.

Mrs. Ninian blew on her tea, into which she had poured a little cognac, against the river damp. "A French lady gave it to me," she said, to no one in particular.

"We're friends; only we don't understand each other well. We don't talk each other's language yet.

"But we will."

14

IF DAVID BELIEVED that the Jews, in time, would understand one another, and share with purpose and courage a common destiny, others in the army did not. And in the weeks preceding the Passover, while they marched in the icy winds along the Khirgiz Steppe eastward toward the black shores of Lake Aral, bitter and endless arguments were held by radicals and conservatives, by the business men of America, and the orthodox saints and scholars of Galicia, who wished the new country to be a religious kingdom under the rule of its priests, like ancient Judah and Israel.

To such Jews as these, dressed in their praying shawls and fringes, to speak seriously of light and power companies, of banks and railroads, seemed

— 165 —

unreasonable and fantastic. Their fathers, and their fathers' fathers before them, had been farmers, scholars, and small shop-keepers; the life of the village was all they knew. "We are God's chosen people," said the Rabbi of Zagreb, to his little congregation. "This is a religion, not a business. Did we come all this way for commercial reasons? Then I am going home again."

On the other hand, when Mr. Alberg, the communist, heard that a company was to be formed to supply the new land with electricity, indignation robbed him of speech. Then he burst out: "It is impossible and I for one will never allow it."

He continued bitterly: "We are many, and they are few, yet already, before we have stopped walking, while we are still shivering and starving in the middle of nowhere, they plan to exploit us. If the socialists were not cowards, and therefore worse than the capitalists, they would help us to defeat such injustice. However, I say that the desert will run red with blood before such a state of affairs can exist again. Besides which, we do not need electric light. What we need, is for everybody to work; and the distribution of wealth."

Gathering together a hundred of his comrades, he made a demonstration in front of the wagons of M. Perez, the banker. Carrying banners and signs on which were printed the words "Down with the Capitalists," and "Socialists We Demand a United Front," the communists paraded slowly across the steppes in the direction of Embinsk.

Full of resentment at the past, they wished to take away from those whom they considered their oppressors, a wealth which no longer existed; and to enjoy for themselves the comforts and advantages which were, at the moment, entirely imaginary.

"Come out," cried Mr. Alberg, shaking his fist at the Perez limousine; "show yourself, rascal and villain."

The automobile, with its blinds drawn, continued to move slowly along the road, driven by the chauffeur from the Department of the Seine, to whom demonstrations were not a novelty. No one appeared at the door, or in any of the other wagons belonging

to M. Perez. His wife, who would have been terri-
fied at the shouts and the brandished fists, was
travelling with Mrs. Ninian, who was teaching her
English; and M. Perez was up front at a meeting of
the council of divisional commanders, to which he
had invited himself in the role of adviser to Mr.
Solomon. Seated in the council wagon, engineers,
lawyers, bankers and economists put their heads
together to consider means of life in the new land.
They carried few supplies with them, and much was
needed; seeds, and tractors, ploughs, cement, wood,
copper and steel, textiles, fertilizer . . . To purchase these materials which were to create cities and
agricultural communities, loans would have to be
negotiated in foreign countries.

There was very little security to offer. But that
did not seem to trouble anybody. M. Perez was convinced that his Paris correspondents would find a
way to deal with such difficulties. And it was pointed
out that in America loans had often been made on
even less security.

"After all," said Mr. Solomon, "we're as good

a risk, taking one thing with another, as the next man."

"Quite," said Lord Steyne; and the ablest jurists of England, France, and the United States agreed with him.

As a matter of fact, the bankers in Berlin had already expressed their indignation at not being offered a share in the business of the new land. "Is it possible," they wrote, "that one can be so unfair?" It was voted to allow them to participate. "Why not?" said Baron Wertheim. "In banking, one does not pay attention to the animosities, one pays attention to the business."

Behind them, the communists were dispersed by troops under the command of a young engineer from the University of Grenoble. Grumbling, they put away their signs, and walked on together, no longer communists, but Jews, and exiles. And Raoul, sat himself down among the sage bushes and the scrub, to wait for the Kovnitz wagons to pass. He hoped to catch a glimpse of Leah, whose father and mother kept her constantly in sight, and with whom he had

exchanged only the most unsatisfactory talks for
more than a month. The dry desert air had brought
color into his thin cheeks, and he smiled to himself.
But after a while, his face took on an expression of
weariness and dissatisfaction. The shapes, the
shadows of exile filed past him on the road, ox-carts,
horses, wagons, an occasional motor, and men and
women on foot, marching along in silence, their eyes
heavy with fatigue, or bright with hunger. The
Kovnitz wagons were not in sight; and Raoul grew
impatient, his longing began to be mixed with
petulance. He thought of the endless leagues behind him, of the countless miles yet ahead; and it
seemed to him that he was wasting the most precious
months of his life, as though body and spirit together were growing thin and dry, deprived of the
meat and drink of love . . . and for what reason?
He struck the palm of his hand with his fist. Because
he was young. But that was the time for love . . .
and soon—he was convinced—he would be young
no longer.

It was always like that, he thought, rebelliously:

first the young were made to suffer for the mistakes of their parents; and then they were denied their share of life's consolations.

No, he cried to himself, why do I wait? I will go to my parents, and tell them, simply, I wish to marry.

I will say: am I to have nothing but hunger and shivering?

But as he rose to go forward in search of his mother, he saw David approaching on the road.

The poet was not alone; he was engaged in conversation with a farmer from the valley of Jezreel, one of those pioneers who had rebuilt the ancient land, only to see it lost again from under him. But he was not discouraged; having reclaimed one desert, he was ready to see what could be done with another.

"Besides," he was saying to David, "it is only for a little while. I do not believe that we have lost Zion; we will return to it some day, when this madness blows itself out in the world. In the meanwhile, what we did long ago with God's help, and again yesterday with the assistance of the English, we can do to-morrow, also with God's help."

They walked along together, discussing the bare and sandy earth over which they were passing. "You are from the Palestine, too?" asked the farmer. "From the land?"

"No," said David; "I am from America, from the city. I am a poet; I do not know how to plough, or to build reservoirs in which to store water."

The member of the Hagganah shrugged his shoulders. "Poets also are useful," he said generously. "And you will learn how to plough."

"Yes," said David gravely, "I will learn." He looked at his hands, thin and sinewy, calloused and dirty. "Why not?" he said.

Seeing Raoul waiting for him at the side of the road, he took leave of his companion with a friendly smile.

"I will ask you to teach me," he said.

"David," exclaimed Raoul, as soon as they were alone, "it is decided; I go at once to my parents, to demand that they make a marriage for me. Must everything wait, because we are refugees? I did not ask to be young, and to be a Jew. What do you think? They will never allow it, probably."

And his face took on an expression of suffering which he really felt.

He wished his friend to encourage him, and to assure him of success. But David thought it would be better to wait until after the Passover. "It will be a time of deep feeling," he said, "because it is the anniversary of the flight from Egypt. We shall be in camp for a week; and there will be services every day. I do not think it is the proper moment to add to the emotions of your parents, and of Leah's father and mother. Wait a little, Raoul; be patient; we still have more than a thousand miles to travel."

"That is the trouble," said Raoul sadly; "before we have gone half the distance, I shall be too old to marry."

Nevertheless in the end, he promised to wait until after the Passover before speaking to his parents. "As always," he said, "you are right. What would I do without you, David? I would be constantly making mistakes of judgment. And perhaps, in the meanwhile, your sainted grandmother might succeed in preparing a little the mind of my mother. Tell her to speak well of my Leah; and of young marriages generally, particularly those of the heart."

And at that moment, catching sight of the Kovnitz wagons, his face lit up with joy. "Goodbye," he said; "you are the best of friends; and everything is all right. Do not let me keep you."

And he drew aside, to let the wagons go by. "I can at least look at my lily of Sharon," he murmured, standing thin, pale, and smiling by the roadside.

15

THE GREAT STEPPES seemed to stretch endlessly
from west to east, a table for the wind which blew at
that season with redoubled force and icy persist-
ence. To the south lay the deserts of Turkestan: but
to the northeast stretched the fertile plains of Asia,
already faintly green with the first weeks of spring,
and toward which Mr. Nieman led his straggling
army of shop-keepers, scholars, farmers, and
musicians.

They were weary; and except for those who were
used to the desert, depressed by their surroundings.
Differences of opinion were exaggerated in the keen
air, which searched out the rags of the poor as well
as the furs of the rich. Along the line of march,
which by this time extended more than a hundred

miles, many private quarrels developed. The communist, Oscar Alberg was attacked by a young socialist and received a bloody nose. At the same time there were many who wished to avoid violence, even by the troops acting as police. And in defence of these views, they grew pale with anger and opposed in a warlike manner those who wished to use force.

Herr Cappellmeister Kamp, late of the Düsseldorf Philharmonik, hunting for hares on the Khirgiz Steppe with his friend the zoologist Professor Baumann, thought of his home in the Rhineland, which the police had ransacked, and of his collection of old scores and musical manuscripts which they had destroyed. What a comfortable little city was Düsseldorf, and how good, plump, and smiling, everybody looked there. He forgot the days of terror and the nights of fear, the tramp of feet on the streets at midnight, the beatings, the cries of the victims, the tearful silence of those who were left behind. He forgot the insults he had received, the humiliations he had endured, he forgot that he had been hurled bodily from the conductor's stand by six brown-shirted soldiers; and he observed to Professor Baumann, "I am homesick for Germany, for my home and that of my fathers before me."

Professor Baumann examined his weapon, which was an old-fashioned slingshot, such as David had used against the Philistines. "You will see it again," he said.

Dr. Kamp continued to elaborate his thought. "Tell me something," he remarked; "do you think I am right to deprive myself of the works of Wagner and Strauss simply because I believe that they do not like me?"

His friend shrugged his shoulders. "Such feelings are beyond me," he declared. "I am not an artist, as you are. However, now that you remind me, I have something I wish to discuss with you. In our division is an American lady, the wife of a delicatessen store-keeper, who expects soon to be a mother. She is exhausted; she needs clothes, and food. I am getting together a fund to provide these things. I will put you down for three marks."

"So many?" asked Dr. Kamp.

"I have already collected seven marks and some roubles," said Professor Bauman simply.

Dr. Kamp's mouth trembled. "I would like to think only of music," he said sadly.

However, that was impossible, for there were disturbances everywhere. In one of the forward divisions, the Reformed congregation of Elberon, New Jersey, was showered with stones by the followers of the Zaddik of Povsk; and Rabbi Mendes Pachecco of Brazil, having declared that only the Portuguese were of pure Jewish blood, received a box on the ear from the broad-nosed Rabbi of Breslau.

At the same time, the German Associations, of which there were several, announced their intention of holding a celebration in honor of the anniversary of the treaty of Frankfort. They were a little late; but they desired an opportunity to parade, with songs and mottoes. When M. Perez, speaking as a Frenchman, protested against this celebration, he was promised some rough handling in the Council. The next day several hundred Germans paraded past the wagons of Baron Wertheim, holding banners on which were inscribed the words: In the soil of the north lie our strong roots.

That night M. Perez wrote his Paris correspondents a long and thoughtful letter; and the Chief Rabbi of Alexandria called in his eastern robes upon Lord Steyne, to pray for peace among the Jews.

When he was finished speaking, the General shook him warmly by the hand. But he did not feel able to give him any other assurances.

The week of the Passover, opening with the Seder evening, fell upon the warring factions like a benediction, and calmed the passions and irritations which had been steadily gathering force. The weather was fair and cold; but in the wind, blowing from the east, it was possible to catch the faintest fragrance of spring, of desert flowers, and warmer streams. The sky of evening, green and clear, lay like a lake of crystal in the west, around the evening star, which, silver as a coin, floated in its depths. The young moon shone with a white and peaceful light; on the bare plains, among the rocks and gorges of the steppe, the candles of the Seder were lighted. The wine was drunk, the unleavened bread broken; and around the fires, in the cold, the families drew together, moved by love and awe, by the melodies of the past, and by the prayers for the future.

"Praised art Thou, O Lord our God," they said; and ate the bitter herbs, and drank the sweet wine.

And from their hearts, overflowing with emotion, with piety, weariness, and dread, they lifted up the prayers of their fathers, of the warriors and saints, the prophets and the martyrs.

"When the Lord turned again the captivity of Zion, we were like them that dream.

"Then was our mouth filled with laughter, and our tongue with singing; then said they among the heathen, The Lord hath done great things for them.

"Turn again our captivity, O Lord, as the streams in the south."

The children questioned; their elders replied. The story of the Passover was told again, in accents of anguish and of love. "Now there arose a new king over Egypt, who knew not Joseph . . ."

They sang the songs of home, they sang the nursery rhymes, the young voices and the old:

"Then came the water
That quenched the fire
That burned the stick
That beat the dog . . ."

It is the night of children, the peace of families rests upon Israel. For a little while their eyes are wide and happy, which have been veiled in mischief, sadness, and doubt. They ask questions, and they are answered; no one bids them be silent, no one bids them return to the loneliness which is the domain of childhood. They join in the songs about the fires, they partake of the life of their elders; they, too, are Israel, the beloved of God. The night of the Egyptians stretches outside; and tomorrow, with its lonely childhood, lies, like the sun, in the east, beyond sleep.

David, too, joined in the old, the unfamiliar songs. With his grandmother, he drank the wine of faith; partaking, with his people, of the fellowship of earth. Around him the Jews were at peace; they belonged on this night to God, and for that reason it was allowed them to be innocent and joyous. They sang; and they remembered the past; they smiled at one another. "We are still here," they said. "God is still here."

Once again the wings of death's dark angel, beating from sky to sky, passed without stooping above the hosts of Jacob, above the tents of the exiles. They had no doors to open to the Messiah; their doors were the doors of night itself, the gates of the hills, the threshold of the winds. The doors of their hearts were open; and with the children, He entered and was at home.

That night the son of Mrs. Cohen was born in the darkness on the Kirghiz Steppe, to the sound of singing, watched by the stars.

16

BEYOND THE BLACK SHORES of the Aral Sea, they were in Asia; there, for the first time, they learned that Europe lay behind them. The Kirghiz tribesmen, the Kazaks of the steppes, rode in on their shaggy ponies, to watch them go by—stout, dark men, in long coats belted about the middle, and laughing women in bright red waists, with silver head-dresses above their braided hair. There the Jews saw for the first time the Mongol yurts and camels of the desert; and turning north, left them behind for the fields and forests of Asia, already green with spring.

Their route lay northward toward Kamenogorsk, then south across the foothills of the Tien Shan, two thousand miles away. As the weather grew warmer, they made better time, and their frozen spirits revived. And as the grass grew long by the roadside, and the little desert flowers gave way to the full-swelling buds and blossoms of the north, they forgot their quarrels, and gave thanks to God for having brought them, if only for a little while, into a land of plenty.

But they were not allowed to linger. The grey-and-red uniformed soldiers of the Soviet hurried them along, and kept a sharp eye out for stragglers.

The winds of spring blew fresh and fair, the sun warmed them, the air was full of fragrance and light. They sang, and joked; the children gathered flowers again by the roadside, and the men called out greetings to the peasants at work in their fields. They thought that because they had survived the winter, they would be more welcome in the world. The Russians did not return their greetings; they leaned on their hoes or their spades, and watched the Jews go by, without saying a word.

Now, in the longer evenings, in the gradual dusk, young men and women walked out together from the wagons, listened to the frogs piping in the marshes, and made their wishes on the first cool star. Once again, around the fires in the sad, damp evenings, the voices of the young girls were heard singing, though more faintly, the songs of their homelands. A breeze of freshness and freedom blew for a little while through the long line of wagons to which had been added some ponies from the steppes, and a few light carts from the Aral district.

Violins were lifted from their boxes, and tuned; stiff fingers were coaxed to move again upon the strings. Betty Solomon's little gramaphone was brought out; it played the tunes of two winters before, on cracked records, and with a thin and quavering sound.

And M. Perez, the banker, shaking his head gloomily with every step, went in search of the Kovnitz Rabbi.

He had argued with Raoul, he had used his authority; he had even wept—to no avail. Raoul was determined to be married, he had talked louder, he had even used more arguments than his father.

And Mme. Perez—of all people—had sided with her son. "Ungrateful woman," exclaimed M. Perez, "how you embarrass me."

Mme. Perez replied: "This is not France any more. Mme. Liebkowitz is an agreeable and sensible woman, of frugal habits. Perhaps, in the new land, the tribe of Kovnitz will have a large representation. I also understand politics, my friend."

That is true, thought M. Perez; and he gazed at his wife in a thoughtful way.

"I already speak a few words of Yiddish," she added. "They do me no harm. Let him marry, if he is set upon it. With such a girl as Leah, any other arrangement is out of the question."

And she concluded in a voice charged with suppressed excitement,

"I cannot allow my son to waste away from emotion under my very eyes."

"And what," asked M. Perez bitterly, "will your son receive from this Polak in the way of a dot? A Torah, and a candlestick."

"You will be surprised," said Mme. Perez

quietly. "A rabbi like the Kovnitzer is in a manner of speaking, a king. He has a treasury."

"Ah," said M. Perez," Hmm. Well . . . a king. Of what?"

And he thought to himself, the sly one, she has already been speaking to Mrs. Liebkowitz.

But he did not relish his task; and he went to see the Kovnitz Rabbi much against his will.

On the other side, the Kovnitzer was even more disturbed than M. Perez, for he could see no benefit to anyone from such a match. "Are we paupers," he asked his wife, "that we should pick up a man from the middle of the road for our daughter? From France; is that a country of the Jews?"

"His father," said Mrs. Liebkowitz mildly, "is a man of great wealth."

The rabbi shrugged his shoulders. "Gold," he said sternly, "is a stumbling block for fools. Is he also a scholar? Can he discuss the Torah, the Mishna, the writing of the saints? What am I to do with such a son-in-law? I know nothing about banking."

And wagging his finger in the air, he added, "It is said, 'Woe unto them who join house to house and lay field to field until there is no place.' And it is said, 'What fellowship shall wolf have with lamb?' "

To this Mrs. Liebkowitz replied, "Mrs. Perez is a good woman, who has taught me a very interesting game with the cards.

"Besides," she added slyly, "a marriage now will have the effect of steadying our Leah, whose wildness has caused us to guard her as the shepherd the lamb."

She was careful not to suggest that it was Raoul to whom Leah had already given her heart. She believed, not unwisely, that the rabbi would be even more vexed were he to learn that Leah and her lover already understood each other.

"When this young man marries," continued Mrs. Liebkowitz inexorably, "he will be able to afford a house with rooms in it for everybody."

"At least," the rabbi admitted, "he is not a communist."

"He is a royalist," replied Mrs. Liebkowitz, "and

he understands that a rabbi is also a king, in a manner of speaking."

"Hmm," said the rabbi; "does he indeed? So. Of course, only in a manner of speaking . . .

"Well . . . let us see what Reb Phineas has to say about all this."

He found the broker drinking tea with the young tailor and others of the Kovnitz congregation. Seated in the fresh green grass, under a tree whose brown, sticky buds were almost ready to burst, they were discussing the question of the weather in heaven; about which the tailor had already expressed the belief that it was always cool, with a distinct flavor of autumn; "Because," he explained, "the robes of the angels, being neither of wool nor yet transparent, are such which would best suit that season of the year." When he saw the rabbi himself bearing down upon them, Reb Phineas got to his feet, and excused himself from his companions. "What is it, Master?" he asked. "What can I do for you?"

Having had the situation explained to him, Reb Phineas promised to attend to everything. "Leave it

to me, Master," he said. "Leave it in my hands. I
will settle everything to everybody's advantage. As
for your daughter, who is worthy of such a jewel?
Nevertheless, I believe that the young man is an excellent match."

And he returned to his friends with an air of excitement. To their questions he returned the answer,
"I have been entrusted with a matter of the greatest
importance. It is said, 'Be not rash with thy tongue,
for God is in heaven and thou upon earth, therefore
let thy words be few.' Which is to say, all in good
time. Let us return to the angels: could not their
robes be proper for the springtime?"

The tailor did not think so. "After the winter is
over," he said, "one still wears woolens, for fear of
taking cold."

Reb Phineas found his task more difficult than he
had expected. For one thing, M. Perez did not wish
to talk to him at all; and for another, they were unable to discover any language which they both understood. "What is this," exclaimed the banker, after
a few minutes, "a broker? I do not need a broker.

When I want a broker, I will tell you. Go away; do me the favor not to annoy me."

Nevertheless, he was finally persuaded to accept the good offices of an interpreter from Cracow.

After the qualities of the bride had been extolled, her rabbinic background, her piety, and her domestic virtues, the question of the settlement arose. Half a dozen times Reb Phineas cried out that all was over, and rose to depart, only to return again with a new suggestion. Vexed and irritated, the banker fumed, coughed, drummed with his fingers, and finally broke out in a shout of annoyance. "What my son hopes to get out of this *mésalliance*, I do not know, I cannot conceive. It is only the prayers of his mother, joined to his own obstinacy, and my weakness, which cause me even to listen to you. But what this young lady will get, on the other hand, is perfectly plain: a young man of refinement, of good family, of sensibility, of moderate wealth . . ."

"What does he say?" asked the marriage broker.

". . . and above all, a man of the world, educated at the university, and with a political future second to none. As the wife of such a man, Mademoiselle will take an important place in the new state, in which her husband, backed by the Credit Lyonnais, can expect to find himself in a formidable position."

Reb Phineas smiled with delight. "What does he say?" he asked the interpreter.

The man from Cracow replied, "He says that it is not enough."

Moved by the sound of the banker's voice, at once austere, and charged with emotion, Reb Phineas exclaimed,

"We will offer him five thousand roubles for this son of his, who does not know how to recite the Kaddish."

The interpreter replied, "He will not take a kopek less than seven thousand roubles."

Reb Phineas gazed up at heaven. "For the man of the world," he murmured, "five thousand six hundred."

"Six thousand five hundred, and he will make the

young lady a present of ten shares in the new electric light company."

In the end, M. Perez agreed to accept on behalf of his son a dowry of six thousand roubles, house linen, and a silver service. And to bind the bargain, he gave Reb Phineas a brooch for Leah, made of silver, and purchased on the Boulevard des Capucines, in Paris.

Reb Phineas returned to the Kovnitz rabbi, very well pleased with himself, and loud in praise of Raoul, with whom he had enjoyed a glass of wine, and who he claimed was a scholar, a saint, and the son of a prince. "This young man has hired me to teach him Yiddish," he said, "and he has before him, besides, a political career of great glory. His father is a man of affairs; when he speaks, the words fall from him as in a torrent, carrying everything before them."

That night Leah did not sleep. She lay awake in her wagon between her mother and father; the flap of the wagon was open, she breathed the sweet air of spring, the fragrance of new grass and flowering shrubs, she heard the singing of men and women around the fires, and the beating of her own heart, which seemed to fill the night with a delicious drumming. The joy of youth, like the sweet smell of clover, penetrated to her bones, and she shivered with love, with excitement, and with a sorrow like pain, obscure and valuable, precious as her dreams, which floated above her like woodsmoke in the night.

The next day Raoul and Leah met, beneath the eyes of their parents, and broke bread together, while the two fathers drank "to life" and to each other, and the mothers wept, exchanging smiles of understanding.

THE GREAT MEADOW lay in a gentle hollow, rising
at its edges to the fringe of woods black as velvet
against the dark night sky in which the moon had not
yet appeared. Warm with the odor of ripening fields,
of forest moss, fungus, and fern, the mid-summer
night pressed down upon the hollow, where thousands had gathered to listen to an orchestra made
up of the most famous musicians in the world.

They lacked tympani, and they had only one horn,
but in the string sections were to be found the greatest virtuosi of their time. Led by Gottfried Kamp,
they performed the works of Wagner, and of Strauss;
and little Sonia Walewska, dressed in pink, with a
ribbon in her hair, played the Mendelssohn, as she
had been promised.

Browned by the sun, thin, intent, the Jews sat about in rows on the dew-wet grass, drinking in the heavenly sounds for which they thirsted. They had dressed themselves up in their best, bringing out of trunks and wooden chests the clothes they had been unable to use on the journey. They had almost forgotten what these were like. . . . They felt strange and shy in front of one another. But at the same time, it helped them to forget the long anguish of the march, to make believe for a little while, that the world was kind to them, giving them music, and the spirit to love it.

It was like a masquerade: dressed as they used to dress, in the cities they had once called home, they dreamt of lighted theaters, of white shoulders and powdered bosoms, of jewels and silks, of ardent glances, and whispered replies.

Dream on, poor wanderers, in your faded clothes, while the moon of Asia floats over you above the misty trees, and the massed violins pour out their song into the wilderness. Dream on, but not for long; winter is not far off, the desert is not far away.

Leah had never heard music like this before, it throbbed in her throat, it spread like wings in her bosom. She scarcely breathed, swept by a tide of longing, blown by a wind of beauty, almost too keen to bear. And Raoul, beside her, watching the moonlight on that sweet, amazed face, thought of the roses of Périgueux, the summer silvery mists of Arles; and with them safe in his heart forever, turned without regret to the desert, beyond the forests, beyond the ever distant hills.

There, too, with Leah beside him, he expected to find joy and grief. Beauty was everywhere for lovers the same; they made all music their own. That tomorrow he might be alive no longer, only served to sharpen his happiness; what he could lose was all the more precious for its fragile mortality. The summer night pressed down upon him, surrounded him with its fragrance, covered him with a mist of moonlight; Tristan's love and death were his, made forever beautiful, teaching lovers everywhere how to die.

At the same time, he did not expect to die; with the optimism of youth, he expected to live, and to make a career for himself. It was Leah who would die; and with sudden terror, he held her close, baffled by the tides of anguish and love which came and went in his heart, like the fragrance of the night, like the shadows of the moon.

Behind him his mother, seated on a bench with Mrs. Ninian, and thinking mistily of Paris, of the music of Ravel, which she had never liked, and of the songs of the music halls, which she had loved, gazed about her without hope at the dark, alien faces among whom she wanted so much to feel at home.

Mrs. Ninian, on the contrary, saw nothing. With eyes tight shut she imagined that Mary was with her, and half in a dream, heard in the music her friend's voice, loving and sweet, and her own replying, murmuring with the flutes and violins:

"Do you remember my wedding? It was in the spring; and the house was full of lilies of the valley."

(Were those lilies, so sweet in the air?)

"Do you remember my Olga, the one who made such good noodle soup? She brought me all her sav-

ings . . . And the good times we had, Frank, before everything happened in the world?"

"Yes, Mary, I remember."

"It's summer where I'm lying, too. There's grass above me. . . . Don't forget me, Frank, don't forget the meadow where you left me."

"I am lonely without you, Mary."

And Mary's voice, faint in the whispering music,

"Under the grass, or in the stony desert, . . . we still have each other, Frank—while you remember."

The thunders of applause for Dr. Kamp sounded like the surf breaking on the shores of the summer beaches where they had spent their youth, or like the roar of cities in which they had grown old.

When little Sonia Walewska appeared before the orchestra, Mrs. Ninian's head was nodding on her breast.

Sonia stood up, small and confident, dressed in pink, her woolly hair brushed in unwilling curls, tied with a blue ribbon. She placed her violin, looking very large, under her chin, stared at the sky, pushed the hair back from around her neck, and waited for the orchestra to begin. She had no doubts about herself; she only hoped that Dr. Kamp would do his best, and that the dampness would not put her out of tune. And she started off in the key of E Minor, with a rush, her bow bouncing a little on the strings.

When she got to the runs and flourishes, her tiny fingers flew, only to grow slow and quiet again, while her stocky body swayed dreamily from side to side, like a little dancer, or a child singing a lullabye to her doll.

At the end of the movement, at which she came out a little breathless, and slightly ahead of the orchestra, the great bowl of the meadow was filled with wave after wave of applause. Here was something the Jews could love, and understand; a child prodigy. She was that mingling of spirit and value, innocence and worth, which satisfied their inmost natures, born to love beauty, and to exchange it for security. Here, already at the age of nine, was an artist, and a bread winner.

But to Ann and Alex, seated on the grass in front

of Ann's parents, Sonia was without charm, a traitor to summer-long, winter-long years of childhood, of concealment, of discontent, a deserter from the ranks of those who warred upon their elders, who fought the losing battles against arithmetic, good manners, and polite conversation. And to Ann, hidden away from glory and applause, lost in the shadow of her own awkward unimportance, Sonia was nothing more or less—so she told Alex—than a loathsome worm.

He agreed with her, charmed with so meaty a description; and they burst out laughing, having, in a single moment, disposed of Sonia, and brought a new word into their lives.

The music bored them; and because they were sleepy, they reminded each other in whispers, in the way of children, of all the funny things they had seen, or heard about. "Do you remember the women we saw with veils over their faces? It's a wonder they wouldn't suffocate, that's what it's a wonder. I'd like to have a veil over me, then people couldn't see me. I think they looked silly. Do you remember those funny men with swords in their boots. No, they were knives . . . Well, knives then. They gave us buttermilk to drink, don't you remember? Oh Alex, the little baby camels, weren't they funny. . . .

"Look—the loathsome worm; her hair ribbon is coming off."

Amanda looked over the heads of the children, at the orchestra and at Sonia. Her eyes were wide and gentle, and filled with dreams. "Why," she thought, "she's only a baby still, and already she has the little gestures of a woman. What a shame, to lose those baby years. . . ."

And turning to her husband, she whispered, "I'm glad that Ann isn't a genius."

Paul nodded absent-mindedly. "Yes," he whispered back. "But I wish she'd learn to swim."

Amanda smiled to herself. Good, active Paul; he had bathed in all the streams, lakes, and rivers on the summer march; his sturdy body rested in the music as in a pool, while his mind swam about like a fish or a seal, urging everybody to be healthy.

Her eyes roamed about, searching for David. She failed to find him, but it didn't matter, she knew that he was there. There was comfort enough in that; and besides, she had nothing, really, to say to him. News of the hospital . . . fewer deaths in the warm weather . . . That wasn't what she wanted to say. She wanted to tell him that she was happy, that all was well with her; that she no longer felt lonely. Summer was summer everywhere the same: the white wild hollyhocks, and wild roses, the bachelor buttons, were like the flowers she had always known; the massed, shining summer clouds, the hot blue summer sky, the long, drowsy evenings loud with katydids and tree toads, spoke to her heart of home. It was not difficult to forget the strangeness in the midst of so much that was familiar. And her love for David, without desire or anxiety, was an ever-present comfort to her, not unlike the cloud by day and the pillar of fire by night which guided the hosts of old across the wilderness, speaking to them of a father's love, assuring them of a father's care. David was there, somewhere, in the dark, in the listening shadows, swept by the same music, drenched by the same moonlight. He spoke the language of her heart, he was like her own people.

"We are not unalike, Amanda. . . ."

Behind her Mrs. Cohen suckled her baby, dreaming of the future, of a land of freedom and a home of peace. "My treasure," she murmured to the tiny dark head pressed against her breast, "my heartbreak, you will never know what it was like, the winter. Drink, drink, with the music, it is good for little stomachs."

And Mr. Cohen, beside her, added proudly to his son, "You too will be a great artist some day. Listen now, and learn how it is done."

At the end of the concerto, Sonia retired amid applause, gratified and serene; the players left their seats, to stretch and rest, and the audience stood up and moved about, talking and greeting one another. The Germans gathered in one corner of the field, elbowing out everybody else; and the broker from Hamburg explained to his friends that at home such a performance as he had just witnessed would not have been tolerated. "But Kamp," he explained, "is a weakling, and without spirit. You can hear it, how he plays Tristan. And what is this, allowing a child to make nonsense on the violin? Let us have no more of it. Let the children remain at home, and learn their lessons."

"There are no lessons," said Professor Baumann drily, "because there are no schools."

"Tscha," replied the broker. And he added angrily:

"Without schools discipline is out of the question."

David sat alone by himself, among strangers. Around him he could see their faces shadowy and dim in the moonlight; in the clothes of the past, in the dresses of happier days, they seemed to exhale a fragrance ardent and tender. Whispers rose and fell about him in the darkness; how many breaths were drawn with joy, with hope, with grief, into those bosoms glowing with life? Jewish men, dreaming and patient; Jewish women, loving and brave, warm and rebellious . . . his love went out to them in the slow, sweet smelling night; he was the lover, the brother and friend, they told their secrets to him, he knew their sorrows, it was for him they wept, he was their joy.

And in turn they held out their arms to him, inviting his youth, inviting his innocence and his longing, gazing at him with affection, with the night-dark gaze of love . . . melting, in music, into infinite pity, into tenderness without end. . . .

No, he thought, I am not sorry any more that I am living in such tragic times. For hearts are most aware of beauty which have suffered most; and beauty is even more beautiful when it looks out at the world through the eyes of courage.

To those whom the world has marked for sorrow, love is the most precious gift of all. Play, then, musician, your music; it is full of life, of longing, and of pain; we listen, it floods us with exquisite joy. None can deny us our share in it, none can withhold beauty from us, for our hearts are open to it, it nestles within them like a homing bird. It is only your words which strike us harsh blows; your music speaks to us in the accents of a brother, and a friend.

Beyond the meadow, in the velvet darkness, under the trees, Benny Abrams lay in Betty's arms, his shorn head pillowed against her breast smooth as the petals of a rose, over her heart which beat with restlessness and with desire, young and rebellious, hostile and afraid.

18

As THE SUMMER ADVANCED, the road turned south,
and the earth, changing her aspect, grew parched
and bare, the landscape barren and formidable. Beyond Kamenogorsk lay the Saizan nor, and beyond
that last wind-darkened lake, China, and the snowy
passes of the Tien Shan. The army passed many
camel trains on the road, led by little grey donkeys,
and laden with silks, tobacco, and uncombed wool
from Sinkiang. The mud and plaster dwellings of
the Russians gave way to Mongol yurts, hung with
colored rugs, and surrounded by frisking goats. The
trees grew sparse; the silver birches drooped and
withered under the enormous sky, in which the summer sun seemed almost not to move. The desert lay
ahead; it stretched out its fingers to them, in desolate

valleys, in brown and winding river-courses, and in the coppery sky, from which the sun beat down with merciless intensity.

Already, camels and yaks had begun to make their appearance in the lines, from which the last of the motors had long since disappeared. As day followed day, and the landscape grew even more unfriendly, a sense of uneasiness made itself felt in the divisions. They were drawing near their goal; the world of which they once had been a part, would soon be forever behind them. Ahead, beyond the last steep and cloudy barrier, lay the desert itself, the lifeless waste, the silent mystery. Less than a thousand miles separated them from their fate; a season's march. They drew together, a brooding anxiety silenced them, they spoke with lowered voices, or not at all; almost as though the desert were listening.

Amanda had been ill, and David went to see her. It took him two days to reach her; he brought her a goat, for which he had exchanged all the wealth he had left in the world. It would give her milk, he told her. She sat, pale beneath her desert tan, languid and feeble, before the tents of the hospital, and looked at him with large, frightened eyes. Her hand in his was cold, for all the heat of the sun. "You were sweet to think of me," she said. "I'll use the milk for Ann; you won't mind, will you?"

And as he said nothing, only looked at her with a warm and steady glance, she added,

"I knew you'd come. It's strange, isn't it. When I was so sick, I was afraid I'd never see you again."

"Here I am, Amanda," he answered.

"Yes," she said. But her mind was still in the past, still going over and over again what had happened to her. "Have you ever been lost in a storm, David?" she asked. "It was like that. It was dark; and I couldn't see you any more. I thought perhaps you'd lost the way. You haven't, have you, David?"

"No," he said, "I haven't lost the way."

She raised his hand to her thin cheek. "Then it's all right," she said. "As long as you know."

He sat with her until evening, while the red sun sank slowly in a haze of dust and heat. They spoke little; there were no words yet for what lay ahead. He gave her his strength, and she gave him her trust. She must draw upon his strength to care for her family; they had nothing else to give each other.

When the first stars shone in the sky, he took his leave of her. She lifted herself up to him, trembling a little, light as a reed; gently then, like children, they kissed each other goodbye. "God keep you," she said. "Thank you for the goat."

He walked all that night, through the moonlight, through mist and shadow and shine. The covered wagons rolled beside him, their tops like little hills of snow under the moon; the slowly moving families spoke together in low voices as he passed. The night spread itself out around him, empty and clear, quiet and wide. He was neither happy nor unhappy; he was at peace, cold and quiet as the night. He wanted to say to God, "Here I am, in case You are looking for me."

At noon the next day he was back in his place in the line; and three days later, Raoul and Leah were married.

The young Frenchman was unwilling to wait any longer for his happiness. "You see," he told David earnestly, "once we start across the mountains, who knows? Perhaps we shall all die in the passes; perhaps none of us will ever reach the Gobi alive. My mind tells me that it is now or never; in agreement with that is my heart; everything is favorable. I wish you to be a witness to my good fortune."

The other three witnesses were to be Oscar Alberg, Manny Jacobs, and Mr. Solomon.

At this time the army marched after sundown, and well into the night, resting during the hottest hours of the day in the shade of the wagons, or a few trees, or rocks. At noon, therefore, Reb Phineas came to prepare Raoul for the ceremony. First of all, he placed around him a garment of white linen such as is worn on the Day of Atonement. Then he called in his parents to give him their blessing.

M. Perez took a stand in front of his son, whom he regarded with a serious expression. Clearing his throat, he remarked: "My child, you are started alone upon a voyage even more severe than this journey to the ends of the earth on which your parents are also embarked. Crises will arise, but I am sure that you will do nothing to make me ashamed of you."

And he added with emotion,

"May God bless you."

Mme. Perez did not wait for him to finish. Throwing herself into Raoul's arms, she exclaimed in a voice choked with tears,

"Your father has forgotten to say that we wish you happiness, my son."

Followed by the four witnesses, and the members of his family, Raoul went to meet Leah. As he passed the wagons of friends and acquaintances, they waved to him, wished him the best of luck, and offered him good advice. They were weary, they did not join the procession; many were already asleep, only too glad to forget, for a little while, the deadening heat which sapped their strength, and the dangers which lay ahead.

An Uzbek family, driving a small camel-caravan northward to Kamenogorsk, stopped to watch, less from curiosity than inertia; they were disappointed in the Jews, whom they had been passing, now, for several days; they thought them dull and uninteresting, but here was something a little different, and possibly worth looking at.

Raoul and Leah, coming from their respective wagons, met under the canopy, the poles of which were held by the young tailor from Kovnitz, his friend the shop-keeper, and two of Leah's cousins from a neighboring village. Already there had been an argument as to which direction the bride and bridegroom ought to face. The young tailor wanted to face to the west, because Jerusalem was in that direction. To this the shop-keeper replied that Kovnitz was also in the west. "Do you wish them to look backward?" he demanded.

"I do not mind facing Kovnitz," replied the young tailor. "I had some very good times in Kovnitz. My grandmother is buried there; and my tailoring establishment also."

At this, one of the cousins, who was a Talmudist, broke in: "When the Jews left Egypt, they turned to the east because that was the direction of the Promised Land. We, also, see our future in the east, beyond the deserts. Let us not turn our faces back toward Jerusalem, of which it is said, 'For Jerusalem is ruined, and Judah is fallen.' "

The endless sun beat down from the copper shield of the sky, the brown and barren landscape quivered like a snake in the heat. But Raoul was cold, with an inner cold which seemed to come from his veins. It was not a chill of fear; the sinews of his purpose, the muscles of his courage seemed to flex themselves, and he shivered. He felt strong and overjoyed, it seemed to him that he was fearless, and impatient to take a firm grip on his foes. It appeared like nothing to build a home, overcome difficulties, and make Leah happy and comfortable. The only trouble was, he wished to begin at once.

"All alone," he exclaimed, "I could attack and vanquish the armies of China, and the robbers of Sinkiang. But probably the day after tomorrow, I will no longer be in the vein."

"To attack and vanquish the robbers among the

ruling class," observed Mr. Alberg, with a glance at Mr. Solomon, "is more important than to fight with a few nomads who, like ourselves, are starving. I agree with you that blood must flow, but I do not believe that it will be Chinese blood."

Under Mr. Alberg's angry eye, Mr. Solomon moved uncomfortably. "Quite," he said. And turning to David, he observed under his breath,

"He is a communist feller."

"We are taking our quarrels with us," said David, "as well as our hopes."

And he looked at Mr. Solomon thoughtfully, as though to say: You, also, have something to learn.

Raoul and Leah stood together hand in hand. Together, in the heat, under the canopy, they faced the rabbi, who said to them: "My children, God, Blessed be He, has brought you here to the edge of the desert, to give you to one another. It is for His glory that He does so . . . nor can we, in our ignorance know what is fitting in the sight of the Most High. It is said, 'As for man, his days are as grass; as a flower of the field, so he flourishes. But the wind passes over, and it is gone.' Yet love is love a thousand years, and from the heart of man and wife arises the fragrance of this immortal word.

"It is said, 'Except the Lord build the house, they labor in vain that build it.' And it is said, 'Lo, the children are from the Lord; and the fruit of the womb is His. Blessed is he that walketh in His ways. His wife shall be a fruitful vine by the sides of his house; his children like olive plants around his table.'

" 'All else is vanity. For one generation goes, and another generation comes; yet the earth abides forever. The sun also rises; and the sun goes down and hastens to his place where he arose. The wind goes toward the south, and turns about to the north; it whirls about continually, and returns again according to its circuits. All the rivers run into the sea, yet the sea is not full; to the places from which the rivers set forth, there they go again.'

"Man also, dutiful and with his love, turns like the wind in its circuits, yet turns again to the place whence he has come, blown by the breath of God backward and forward across the earth.

"May he be no less humble than the streams which water the fields, turning again with patience to their sources, leaving in the valleys below their moisture, and in the meadows, their benediction.

"Blessed art Thou, O Lord, King of the universe. To Thee I now commend this youth and this maiden, standing before me; may peace shine like a light in their house, may the sound of their voices be low and happy, may their hearts not part from one another. And may they in the fulness of time, fructify the earth with children, according to Thy will, of which it is said, 'Yea, thou shalt see thy children's children, and peace upon Israel.'"

Led by Reb Phineas, Leah walked seven times around her husband, cradling him within the whiteness of her body, turning about him like the universe of stars and planets, which to his heart, she was. Her dreams wove him in: as she walked, she spun from out her love a web pure as the color of white, lighter than spider's silk; and drew him into it, forever.

The contract was read, the wine drunk, the glass

shattered; and to the strains of a fiddle, and with beating hearts, Mr. and Mrs. Raoul Perez went arm in arm to their new home among the Kovnitz wagons.

19

THE HEAT GREW MORE INTENSE, the plain more
parched and desolate. Only the locusts sang, from
the dried beds of the streams. In the heat, as in the
cold, the Jews turned sullen; they sickened of
dysentery, they lacked food, and such water as they
found to drink made them even more feeble than
before. Sickness made its appearance in the camps,
claiming many victims. Some gave way to apathy,
or despair; but others were bitter in their misery,
and looked about for somebody to blame. Among
them was the delicatessen store-keeper's wife, Madelon Cohen.

Her child was wasting away in her arms; and she
was beside herself with anxiety and grief. "You said
there would be milk," she told her husband. "You

said everywhere were cows. It is the rich who have the milk. They are like vultures who feed upon our dying children, while you stand there without saying anything."

And she continued in this strain.

Hyman Cohen sat for a long time in the heat, without speaking. Then all at once he jumped up, and went in search of Baron Wertheim. When he came within sight of the wagons of the banker, he brandished his fist and shouted,

"You are stealing our milk. Give it back, because my child is dying."

Poor Baron Wertheim, he had no milk to give anyone, not even enough for himself; it was not his fault that he had been born rich, and a banker. Where he had come from, they had needed bankers in the world. He closed the flaps of his wagon, and sat there alone, in the dark. His spirits were at a low ebb.

Bareheaded in the intense sun, Mr. Cohen felt giddy, and at the same time nothing was too much for him. Soon his shouts had attracted to him a crowd of several hundred men and women. Then he wished to sit down and talk; he was tired, and in addition, he had never had so many friends before. But he could not get anybody to listen to him; for everybody was talking at once, and fists were being raised and shaken at the wagons in which no one was to be seen.

After a while the mob moved away again, without doing anything. Hyman Cohen went with it. He kept trying to enter into conversation with the men around him. "I have a son," he told them. "He is going to be a great fiddler some day. Music, that's the thing. Are you perhaps a socialist? What a time we had in Russia, freezing every minute. It was on the Passover that my son was born. And now we are dying of heat. Well, that's the way it goes."

The man at his side paid no attention to him. Seizing a stone, he brandished it in the air. "Down with the rich," he cried. "We will take their money away from them."

That night the radicals gathered in the cold and silent plain, in the darkness beyond the camp-fires.

But Baron Wertheim sent post haste for Lord Steyne; and for such friends as he had among the socialists, who alone might be expected to defend him, if not for his sake, then for their own. They gathered near his wagons in the darkness; they had no love for the communists.

And when, at dawn, armed with clubs, knives, and a few old pistols, the communists moved in a body on the banker's wagons, they found themselves opposed not by the soldiers, but by others like themselves, who had gathered to dispute their way.

It was not what the communists had expected; but it suited them just as well. There, by the Irtysh River, on the brown plain, almost within sight of the distant crystal peaks of the Tien Shan, the two hosts faced each other like Ephraim and Gilead of old; and like those warring tribes, whose differences of blood and opinion were so slight, and whose hostility to each other was so great, stood in silence and listened to the speeches of their leaders.

They listened also, but with less enthusiasm, to the words of Rabbi Hart, who begged them in a voice hoarse with emotion, to return quietly to their places, and continue the march without shedding the blood of men as weary and as unhappy as themselves.

The delicatessen store-keeper was among the communists, where he did not belong. For a while, it did not seem very important to him; shivering with excitement and fever, he only wished to fight on one side or the other. But as the morning drew on, he grew weary of his companions, most of whom were young and surly, and who did not wish to talk to him. Seeing, across the way, faces he knew, he pushed his way to the outskirts of the throng around him, and started to cross the empty plain between the two armies.

Unaware of his intentions, a number of young men followed him. They thought it was a charge, or an attack; and jumped into the air with shouts. Each imagined himself a David or a Joab. At the sight of this advance, the socialists drew together in dismay; then encouraged by their own numbers, they prepared to resist. When Mr. Cohen reached their lines, he was met by a blow which stretched him upon his back. Struggling to his feet again, and gazing about him in astonishment, he found himself in the midst of a battle.

Dr. Hart was also in the mêlée; but only to argue with the combatants. He still implored them to stop, and to go home; he pleaded with them not to destroy, in a moment of blind fury, the effort of so many months. His shirt was ripped from his back and he was finally rescued by the soldiers, covered with bruises, and breathing with difficulty.

Lifting his arms above his head, he exclaimed bitterly: "This is like the wars of the tribes. It is like the pool of Gibeon, and the ford at the Jordan. We are back at the beginning again. All is lost."

And he let his hands fall to his sides with a gesture at once tragic and resigned.

Lord Steyne, grey and quiet, gave his orders in a dry voice. He knew that there was nothing to be done; that only death or exhaustion would quiet these hearts raging and boiling like the sea. Hating each other more for their likeness than their differences, socialists and communists attacked each other with incredible fury. In the glare of the sun, in the red dust rising like a fog in the air, they peered at each other like enemies, above fists, clubs, and knives. All the long-hidden despair at their fate, all the fear and weariness of the march, pressed itself out in shrieks and blows, in a battle, in which arms and legs were broken, heads smashed, and men and women hurled down and trampled in the dust.

Oscar Alberg was in the thick of it. It hardly mattered to him whom he fought; his heart beat with joy to feel each blow that he gave—even to feel the blows he took himself, to feel pain changing into rage as it entered his body. He felt strong, and alive; he was the lion of Judah, the captain of a host. Gone was the Oscar Alberg of the speeches, of the arguments; in his place stood a warrior, raging through the fight, giving back to the world with all his strength the injuries he had received. That this world consisted only of poor people, like himself, never even occurred to him. He did not stop to think whose head rolled cracked and muddy at his feet. He was

Jephthah at the passage of the Jordan, he was Joab at the pool of Gibeon.

And when, in turn, a stranger's knife flew upward, passing through the muscles of his belly, he bowed himself still in a kingly glory, still in a mist of joy, to join those others, the poor and sorrowful, over whom the world had long since passed with a sound of thunder, like the tide of battle rolling above him, fainter and fainter in his dying ears.

His hand, relaxed in death, lay like a leaf across the face of little Mr. Cohen, the delicatessen storekeeper. Mr. Cohen's blue eyes, under his cracked skull, were dim and peaceful; he had forgotten his troubles, he had forgotten everything. He walked with Madelon in green and flowering pastures; they were welcome there, no one wished to keep them out.

His lips moved, and made no sound. But in his mind he was telling Madelon that everything would be all right some day. He was saying that in the new land people would be free to love one another. "Do not cry any more," he was saying, "or be afraid. Where we are going, there will be milk for the baby, and a new dress for you. There is enough for everyone, in the world. It is only that the rich must give up a little of what they have.

"Look—everything is green, and there are flowers. Do not be afraid for the child, Madelon. He will grow up in his own land, where everybody will be friends."

The blue eyes closed; the thin, failing hand reached out and patted Mr. Alberg's cold cheek. "Goodnight," he whispered, "Madelon. Soon everything will be all right."

Over him, in the red dust, the bodies heaved and swayed more slowly; weariness, taking its toll, was making room for horror. Over the clenched fists, faces no longer seemed distorted by rage, but set in lines of despair. "Who are you?" they seemed to ask each other: "What has happened? What are we doing to each other?"

It was for this moment that Lord Steyne had been waiting. Quietly, the troops went in among the rioters, and led them out one by one, stumbling and sobbing, or dazed and still. Like children, they were glad to give themselves up to authority again, after the nightmare of temper. . . . They left behind them the dead and the dying, watched from the sky by the kites, who soared out across the plain from the haze veiling the distant peaks, aloft in the darkening heavens.

Evening drew on; for a moment, in the blue, misty air, the white peaks of the Tien Shan stood out like clouds far off, low in the eastern sky. Then the night, which was over China, moved westward across the earth, across the desert and the passes, across the cooling plain, where by the light of torches the burial parties moved among the slain, and men and women crouched, seeking their dead.

In his tent by the river, Dr. Hart wept, and would not be comforted. But Lord Steyne, stopping off for a moment to see Mr. Solomon, remarked,

"Now we shall have peace for a while."

"I'm glad of that," said Mr. Solomon.

THE PEARLY LIGHT of morning filled the sky, wash-
ing the earth from pole to pole, when David awoke,
and went to hitch his shaggy pony to the wagon. He
stood for a moment drinking in the fresh desert air
chilled by the distant snows, stretching his arms and
yawning. His grandmother was already awake, the
kettle, heated on a fire of rushes, was boiling. He felt
rested, and alert. Behind him Raoul's wagon, silent,
motionless in the morning mists, seemed to emerge
full of secrets, from the night. In the distance in the
direction of the Irtysh River, he heard the cries of
kites, circling in the air. The day, so early, so cool,
was full of peace.

Far off, low on the horizon, faint as clouds, lay
the piled masses of the Tien Shan, barely visible—

the last great wall, behind which stretched the endless wastes, in which the dinosaurs had died, and to which the Jews now addressed themselves. In his mind, David saw them, the long brown columns marching wearily across the land, disappearing into the distance over the slow blue curve of the world . . . the last hills, beyond which history did not go, against whose sheer and crystal summits the winds of the past blew in vain to cross.

We must do what history cannot do, thought David; we must pass where storms cannot follow.

He returned to the wagon, where Mrs. Ninian was making her preparations for the start. "It is time to go," he said. "You can see the hills."

Was it Amanda's voice he heard, faint and loving? *"I thought perhaps you'd lost the way. You haven't, have you?"*

"No, I haven't lost the way."

Quietly, as one who does what she must, Mrs. Ninian packed the wagon for the day's journey, setting everything in order.

"I'm ready, David," she said.

Behind them the moon, over the full, and following the night, floated down the western sky, silver as a cloud against the deepening blue. And the sun, as they started, rose red and glowing in the east, out of the haze which covered the mountains. The day swept down upon them; its light shone in their eyes as they went forward.

A NOTE ON THE TYPE IN WHICH THIS BOOK IS SET

This book is composed on the linotype in Bodoni, so called after Giambattista Bodoni (1740–1813), son of a printer of Piedmont. After gaining experience and fame as superintendent of the Press of the Propaganda in Rome, Bodoni became in 1766 the head of the ducal printing house at Parma, which he soon made the foremost of its kind in Europe. His Manuale Tipografico, completed by his widow in 1818, contains 279 pages of specimens of types, including alphabets of about thirty foreign languages. His editions of Greek, Latin, Italian, and French classics, especially his Homer, are celebrated for their typography. In type-designing he was an innovator, making his new faces rounder, wider, and lighter, with greater openness and delicacy. His types were rather too rigidly perfect in detail, the thick lines contrasting sharply with the thin wiry lines. It was this feature, doubtless, that caused William Morris's condemnation of the Bodoni types as "swelteringly hideous." Bodoni Book, as reproduced by the Linotype Company, is a modern version based, not upon any one of Bodoni's fonts, but upon a composite conception of the Bodoni manner, designed to avoid the details stigmatized as bad by typographical experts and to secure the pleasing and effective results of which the Bodoni types are capable.

THIS BOOK WAS COMPOSED BY VAIL-BALLOU PRESS, INC., BINGHAMTON, N. Y., AND PRINTED AND BOUND BY H. WOLFF ESTATE, NEW YORK. THE PAPER WAS MADE BY P. H. GLATFELTER CO., SPRING GROVE, PA.